FROM GENESIS
TO THE
DIAMOND SUTRA

A WESTERN BUDDHIST'S
ENCOUNTERS WITH CHRISTIANITY

SANGHARAKSHITA

WINDHORSE PUBLICATIONS

Published by Windhorse Publications Ltd
11 Park Road
Birmingham
B13 8AB

Cover design Satyadarshin
Produced by Bookchase UK Ltd, London
Printed and bound in the EU
L.D.: SE-3136-2005
A catalogue record for this book is available from the British Library

ISBN 10: 1 899579 72 9
ISBN 13: 978 1 899579 72 3

Contents

	Preface	1
Chapter One	Early Memories	5
Chapter Two	The Bible as Literature	17
Chapter Three	The Church	31
Chapter Four	The Apostles' Creed	49
Chapter Five	Christian Mythology	71
Chapter Six	Christian Ethics	97
Chapter Seven	Saints and Mystics	119
Chapter Eight	Jesus	139
Chapter Nine	Barlaam and Josaphat	153
Chapter Ten	Buddhism and Christianity	167
	Index	173

ABOUT THE AUTHOR

Sangharakshita was born Dennis Lingwood in South London, in 1925. Largely self-educated, he developed an interest in the cultures and philosophies of the East early on, and realized that he was a Buddhist at the age of sixteen.

The Second World War took him, as a conscript, to India, where he stayed on to become the Buddhist monk Sangharakshita. After studying for some years under leading teachers from the major Buddhist traditions, he went on to teach and write extensively. He also played a key part in the revival of Buddhism in India, particularly through his work among followers of Dr B.R. Ambedkar.

After twenty years in India, he returned to England to establish the Friends of the Western Buddhist Order in 1967, and the Western Buddhist Order in 1968. A translator between East and West, the traditional world and the modern, and between principle and practice, Sangharakshita's depth of experience and clear thinking have been appreciated throughout the world. He has always particularly emphasized the decisive significance of commitment in the spiritual life, the paramount value of spiritual friendship and community, the link between religion and art, and the need for a 'new society' supportive of spiritual aspirations and ideals.

Sangharakshita recently handed on most of his responsibilities to his senior disciples in the Order. From his base in Birmingham, he is now focusing on personal contact with people, and on his writing.

PREFACE

IT WAS MY INTENTION SOME YEARS AGO to write a full-length comparative study of Buddhism and Christianity, but old age, and therewith the partial loss of my eyesight, have crept up on me and prevented me from carrying out this plan, which in any case was an ambitious one. I was unwilling, however, to give up the idea altogether, and it occurred to me that if I was unable to produce a full-length comparative study of the two religions I could at least write an account of my personal contact, over the years, with Christianity and Christians.

Thus the present work is largely autobiographical, though I have not hesitated to deviate, from time to time, from the autobiographical framework in order to explore an aspect of Christianity which was of special interest to me. I have written it for my own satisfaction. I wanted to take stock, as it were, of my attitude to Christianity as it had impinged on my life and thought in the course of the last eighty years. At the same time, I wanted to share my experience, and my reflections on my experience, with those Western Buddhists who, like me, grew up within a Christian culture, as well as with students of comparative religion, and with Christians who might be interested to know how one modern Buddhist, at least, in retrospect views their religion.

After relating my early memories of Christianity and Christians in chapter one, I turn my attention, in chapter two, to the Bible, especially to the poetical books of the Old Testament, which I enjoyed as a boy and which I still enjoy. The fact that I am a Buddhist does not in the least detract from my enjoyment of

1

them, for I read the Bible as literature, not as the Word of God. In chapter three, beginning with the Gunpowder Plot, the anniversary of which I celebrated as a small boy, and ending with the persecution of the Vietnamese Buddhists by the ruling Catholic oligarchy, I trace the way in which power has corrupted the Roman Catholic Church. I also relate my contact with Catholic priests, one of whom became a good friend.

In chapter four I take a look at the Apostles' Creed, for it is this ancient formula which constitutes the basis of mainstream Christianity, whether Roman Catholic, Lutheran, Anglican, or Orthodox in its form. I wanted to make clear, to myself, and hopefully to others, the fundamental difference between Buddhism and Christianity. Even in the Creed there are elements I can accept, provided they are understood as myths and symbols, not as literal truth. The orthodox Christian believer regards the doctrine of the Virgin Birth as being a statement of historical fact. The Buddhist scriptures certainly contain myths and legends, but they form no part of Buddhist doctrine, and the individual Buddhist is free to accept or reject them as he or she pleases. Chapter five is devoted to what I call Christian mythology, which is for me, at least in the form it has assumed in the Western Church, the product of the Catholic collective imagination. In this chapter, as in several others, I give expression to my appreciation of, and delight in, some of the masterpieces of Christian art. I also critique, in connection with the figure of Satan, the twin notions of absolute evil and irremeable reprobation.

In chapter six, which deals with Christian ethics, I describe two incidents in my early childhood which were responsible for the awakening in me of a distinctly moral consciousness. This leads me to a consideration of violence, especially the violence that Christianity has regularly directed against heretics and homosexuals. I express myself strongly in this connection. It certainly was not my intention to offend any Christian, but there are elements in Christianity which I cannot but regard with horror, not just as a Buddhist but as a moral being. In the context of this chapter 'homosexuality' means male homosexuality, the Church for some reason being much less fierce against lesbianism, despite Leviticus and St Paul. The saints and mystics who are the subject of chapter seven were all remarkable personalities, and their lives are of great human interest. In their different ways they all made a strong impression on me, and it is for this reason that I have written about them.

After the saints and mystics comes Jesus, who figures in chapter eight. In this chapter I tell how I oscillated, over the decades, between believing and not believing in his historical existence. These doubts did not prevent me from being deeply moved by paintings of his life, some of which I describe. I also discuss the Christology of Marcion, a 'heretical' teacher of the second century, and comment on a novelistic reconstruction of the gospel story by a great Irish writer – a reconstruction I found both plausible and appealing. Chapter nine is devoted to the legend of Barlaam and Josaphat, which may be regarded as a sort of bridge between Buddhism and Christianity. In this chapter I trace the steps by which a traditional Indian biography of the Buddha was gradually transformed into the story of two Christian saints, one of whom – St Josaphat – is quite recognizably the Buddha. In the last chapter I ask myself what I have learned by immersing myself in Christianity for the nine months it took me to produce this book.

I would like to thank Jnanasiddhi for her helpful editorial suggestions, and Shantavira for his meticulous copy-editing, for which I have often had cause to be grateful. Above all, I would like to thank my friend Nityabandhu, to whom I dictated the whole book, and without whose cooperation it would not have seen the light.

Sangharakshita
Birmingham
26 April 2005

Chapter
one

Early Memories

I AM A BUDDHIST. I have been a Buddhist for more than sixty years. But I was born to nominally Christian parents in a country where Protestantism in its Anglican form was the established religion, and in a part of the Western world where Christianity had been for centuries the dominant religious and cultural influence.

My first contact with Christianity took place a few days after my birth on 26 August 1925, when I was baptized in St Nicholas Parish Church, Tooting Graveney, wearing the same christening veil in which my father had been baptized 27 years before. What may have been my second contact with Christianity was also connected with my father. It was he who taught me at a very early age the prayer which his maternal grandmother had taught him when he himself was a child. The prayer ran:

> When I lay me down to sleep
> I pray the Lord my soul to keep.
> If I should die before I wake
> I pray the Lord my soul to take.

Why my father taught me this prayer I cannot say, but he told me I should repeat it every night before I went to sleep, probably because I slept alone and was subject to nightmares. The worst of these nightmares occurred only once. Towering above me I saw in the darkness an enormous black wooden cross. It rose up out of a kind of black wooden maze or labyrinth, and the atmosphere was one of indescribable gloom, horror, and dread.

My father was very fond of his old grandmother, having lived with her in her Norfolk village after the premature death of his father. It was she who had given him, apparently, what was known in the family as Grandmother's Bible. This was a massive volume with a tooled leather cover and a worn gilt clasp, and its richly coloured illustrations of such subjects as Daniel in the lion's den and Samson rending the lion must have been the first religious pictures I saw. In our home there were no religious pictures, though in the passage between my room and my parents' bedroom there were small reproductions of Rossetti's *Dante's Dream* and Holiday's *Dante and Beatrice*. Ours was in fact not a religious family. My parents went to church only once every two or three years, nor did they ever discuss religion, and his teaching me his grandmother's prayer was the only religious instruction I ever received from my father.

I did of course have godparents, who by sponsoring me at the time of my baptism had made themselves responsible for my religious education. My godparents were my father's sister Helen and Thomas Whitehead, an old friend of the family, but though I saw both of them frequently (Uncle Tom, as I called him, lived across the road) neither of them ever gave me even as much religious instruction as I had received from my father when he asked me to repeat his grandmother's prayer every night. The only person on my father's side of the family who could be described as at all religious was his mother, widowed for the second time, who at least attended church regularly and who, when I reached the age of fourteen, was vaguely troubled that I was not being confirmed.

On my mother's side of the family things were hardly better. The only one who took religion seriously was Uncle Jack, her youngest brother but one, who lived in Tooting Bec and who, with his wife Hilda, was a fairly regular visitor to our house, as we were to theirs. A gentle, kindly man with a nervous manner and a fondness for lavatorial humour, he had been for many years a Sunday School teacher. It was he who presented my sister Joan and me with our first Bibles, for besides being our uncle he was her godfather. Later I gathered, from conversations I happened to overhear, that he had formerly been very religious indeed. He had been in the habit of falling on his knees in the High Street and calling upon people to pray. At family gatherings, moreover, he would hold forth on the subject of religion until told to shut up by his four unsympathetic sisters, who attributed his religious mania – as they saw it – to the fact of his having been shell-shocked while serving in the artillery during the Great War. Despite the fact that she was accustomed to join with her sisters in 'shutting up' poor Uncle Jack, Auntie Kate, my mother's eldest sister, who was a great favourite of mine, as I was of hers, was not wholly indifferent to religion. Unlike the rest of the family, she did not belong to the Church of England. She was a Roman Catholic, having married an Irishman at an early age, and a little of his ancestral faith seems to have rubbed off on her. Once she gave me a tiny medal that had been blessed by the Pope, and on a later occasion, when my mother and I accompanied her to Westminster Cathedral, she lit a candle in front of one of the altars and knelt down and said a prayer.

Though they hardly ever set foot inside a church, my parents sent my sister and me to Sunday School every week. This was due partly, I imagine, to the fact that as children *they* had been sent to Sunday School, and partly in order that they might have an hour or two to themselves on Sunday afternoons. Joan and I went not to St Nicholas but to the octagonal Congregational Church, which was much nearer, where we sat on a hard bench against the wall, in the bottom class, feeling bored, and from which we returned clutching little coloured pictures illustrative of various Bible scenes. It was at this church that I attended my first service, at which I saw the Holy Ghost, as I told my astonished parents on returning home. They eventually came to the conclusion that what I must really have seen was the minister in his white surplice, but I have since wondered if that was the explanation. Perhaps I had had an experience similar to those that came upon me, six or seven years later, at Amen Corner, and as I was walking from Amen Corner in the direction of Tooting Broadway. In any case, I'm not sure whether ministers of the Congregational

Church do, in fact, wear surplices like their Anglican counter-parts.

At the same time that I was attending Sunday School I was also attending the Selincourt Road Infant School, to which I started going – most reluctantly – when I was four. Besides the three R's, the curriculum included Scripture, though lessons in this subject may not have begun for a year or two. 'Scripture' meant the Bible, particularly the parables of Jesus, which our teacher read to us from the New Testament or told us in her own words. We also repeated the Lord's Prayer at morning assembly and sang such hymns as 'All Things Bright and Beautiful' and 'Away in a Man-ger'. How deep an impression all this Religious Education, as it would now be called, made on me, I cannot tell. I absorbed words and phrases – even stories – but did not, I think, acquire any definite conceptions.

So far, there was little that was unusual about my story. Except for my 'seeing the Holy Ghost', it was the story of thousands of South London boys of my generation and class. But when I was eight, and had just started junior school, there took place in my life a sudden and violent change – a change that affected, directly and indirectly, the whole future course of my existence. I was diagnosed as having valvular disease of the heart and was con-fined to bed. There I spent two years or more, forbidden visitors, and unable to do anything except read.

Fortunately – for I soon worked my way through my father's small collection of books – a friendly neighbour gave me a com-plete set of Harmsworth's *Children's Encyclopedia*, which quickly became my constant and much-loved companion. As I wrote forty-five years ago:

> All sixty-one parts (including the Index) were at my
> bedside day and night, and rarely was I seen without one
> of them in my hand. Thanks to Mr Harmsworth I was no
> longer alone in my little room with the nasturtium-
> patterned wallpaper, the owl clock, the model yacht, and

my one dozen oft-read volumes. I could now speak with the good and wise of all ages; I could follow Nature into her innermost recesses and explore all her secrets, from the constitution of the heavens to the structure of a crystal. The pageant of history from its first dawnings in Egypt, China, and Babylonia, passed with all its kings and princes, its priests and nobles and common people, before my eyes. The buskined and unbuskined heroes of ancient and modern tragedy trod my bedside rug for their stage. Perseus slew Medusa the Gorgon, Hercules performed his Twelve Labours, and Jason went in search of the Golden Fleece in my sight. Shining presences of marble and bronze rose as though to music and stood before me in the naked glory of their perfectly proportioned Hellenic manhood; pensive Italian Madonnas smiled. The cross on which Christ was crucified, the tree beneath which the Buddha attained Enlightenment, had their roots in the floor of my room, wherein, as into a garner, the harvest of the ages was gathered unto me for the making of the bread that would keep my soul alive. The body was forgotten, and my imagination, now possessed of 'infinite riches in a little room', rejoiced in the freedom of all the heavens of the spirit.

The contact that I had with Christianity in the course of my immersion in the *Children's Encyclopedia* was largely mediated by the latter's numerous reproductions of Christian works of art or, at least, of paintings depicting scenes and personages from the Old and New Testaments, the lives and legends of saints, angels, and important events in ecclesiastical history. In later years I saw not a few of these paintings with my own eyes in Italy, Germany, and Spain, as well as in the museums and art galleries of my native land. There were also pictures of Gothic cathedrals, stained glass windows, and illuminated manuscripts. From the simply written articles I learned, moreover, about the Bible, about the Crusades and the Inquisition, about reformers like Luther and Calvin, and about such masterpieces of Christian literature as *The Pilgrim's Progress* and *Paradise Lost*. In one of the sections devoted to poetry I came across some excerpts from the latter. The reading of these sowed in me a lifelong admiration for Milton's poetic presentation of the great Christian myth, which begins with the Creation and Fall of Man, culminates in the Crucifixion, and concludes with the Last Judgement. What was more important still, I learned from the *Children's Encyclopedia* that Christianity was not the only religion in the world. There were Buddhism and Hinduism, Taoism and Confucianism, Zoroastrianism and Islam, all of which possessed millions of adherents and had given rise to great civilizations and cultures.

When the days of my incarceration came to an end, my attention naturally was again directed to the outer world, from which I had so long been cut off. But this time it was not directed to that world more or less exclusively, as previously had been the case. The world of ideas and the imagination was now no less real to me than was the world of sights and sounds. In a way it was more real to me, for there were times when the people I saw from the wheelchair in which, for six or seven months, I was pushed around Tooting, were as phantoms compared with some of those I encountered in books. My two years in bed had brought about a permanent change in my character, outlook, and interests, a change that may not otherwise have taken place, at least not so early in my life. Henceforth I was to live in two worlds, one that I shared with others, one that was all my own. Inasmuch as they possess reflexive consciousness, all human beings live in two worlds, but whereas most people lived much more in the outer world of sights and sounds than in the inner world of ideas and the imagination, with me it was the precise opposite. With me, moreover, the imbalance between my two worlds was far greater than it generally is in the case of those who are labelled introverts, and so remained for some time.

On my being allowed to give up the wheelchair and walk, though not to run or play games, I not only went back to school but soon joined the Boys' Brigade. From then on, my contact with Christianity took place not just through the medium of books but through the connection I formed with its institutions and its official and unofficial representatives, for the Boys' Brigade was a Protestant organization, each of its companies being affiliated to the local Protestant church and having that church's minister as its colonel. I was a member of the Boys' Brigade for nearly four years, donning its uniform for the Friday evening parade, when our little company was drilled by its 'officers', taking part in the Wednesday evening prayer meeting and the Sunday morning Bible class, and, eventually, attending the Sunday morning and evening services at the Baptist church to which our company was affiliated. The pastor of the church was Mr Rudman, a sandy-haired man in his mid-thirties whose sermons, which were on the long side, were aimed at the heart rather than at the head, generally left his congregation feeling deeply moved. The members of the church with whom I had greatest personal contact were short, sprightly Mr Ovey, the captain of our company, who liked to be addressed as 'Skipper', elderly, grizzled Mr Young, one of the sidesmen, who plied me with little books of daily Bible readings and who once expressed his conviction that the Lord had chosen me for a great work. There was also the much younger Reg, the company's lieutenant, who drilled us in Mr Ovey's absence, and the still younger Ben, who after giving us tea at his house, two or three at a time, invited us to go down on our knees and offer up our souls to Jesus, which out of politeness we duly did.

They were all good people, and I liked and respected them, but I could not share their simple faith nor, so far as I remember, did the contact I had with them contribute to the development of my religious convictions. I might return home after a particularly moving sermon by Mr Rudman with my heart overflowing with love for the person of Christ, but at night, when I said my prayers, I did not say them only to him. As my habit was at this period, I said them to the Buddha, Christ, and Muhammad in turn, thus hedging my bets in a way that went one better than Pascal and his famous wager. Membership of the Boys' Brigade satisfied my societal instinct, my need to belong to a group, but the church to which our company was affiliated could not meet my need for something more than a temporary emotional exaltation. Even at the weekly vestry prayer meeting, the sort of evangelical equivalent to the Anglican confirmation class, which after a couple of years I was invited to join, less emphasis was placed on doctrine than on devotion, though we did once study Bunyan's *The Holy War* with a speaker from another church, and I did have one serious argument there. This argument was about salvation. Tommy, a boy of my own age, maintained that salvation was by faith alone, whereas I declared that salvation was by faith and works.

On 3 September 1939 I went to church as usual, having just attended Bible class in the adjacent hall. Only one hymn had been sung when there was a dramatic interruption to the proceedings. As I wrote twenty years later:

> A sidesman ascended the pulpit steps and handed the pastor a slip of paper. Slowly rising to his feet, the pastor announced, not the number of the next hymn, but the fact that our country was at war with Germany. Adding that members of the congregation would no doubt wish to return as quickly as possible to their homes, with a short prayer and a blessing he dismissed us. As we left the church the first air raid warning sounded.

Less than a year later, the 'phoney war' having come to an end, with other boys from the Ensham Central School, which I had been attending for the last year or more, I was evacuated to Devon. This was a change which, even if it was not so sudden as the one that had occurred six years earlier, was hardly less violent. It was also of an exactly opposite nature. Instead of being confined to bed, seeing only my parents, the doctor, and the district nurse, I was sent to a distant, unfamiliar part of the country to live, at first as a not very welcome evacuee, among people who were not just strangers but strangers whose ways, in certain respects, including their habits of speech, were very different from those to which I was accustomed. The change also brought about an extension of my contact with Christianity. In Barnstaple, the North Devon town to which I was evacuated, I was billeted first with a grey-haired Anglican clergyman and his elderly aunt and uncle, then with a Church-hating Wesleyan Methodist and her two small sons, and on Sundays attended their respective places of worship. I was greatly struck by the difference – in furnishings, in atmosphere, and in the type of service – between the little parish church with its more traditional style of architecture, where my host conducted the service and preached, and the big barn-like Wesleyan chapel. One, I felt, was a sacred place, while the other was not.

In Torquay in the south, where I ceased to be an evacuee, and where I left school and started working, my contact with Christianity was further extended. To please my grandmother, then staying with Uncle Charles, my father's half-brother, who had been evacuated to Torquay with his firm, I sometimes accompanied her to the little corrugated-iron Anglican church she was attending at that time. One Sunday the dignified, ascetic-looking old priest who was in charge preached on the text 'And every several gate was of one pearl' from the Book of Revelation. I do not remember what he said, but the image of gates that were 'one pearl' remained firmly lodged in my mind. Once I went to St Mary's, the local parish church, with Auntie Kath, Uncle Charles' lively and intelligent wife. Both Anglican churches were decidedly High Church, especially St Mary's, where there was incense and music, and where the service concluded with a grand procession round the church, complete with processional crosses and embroidered banners, surpliced choristers walking two and two, and priests in unusually colourful vestments. Auntie Kath loved all this, and I saw that ritual had a place in religion, especially popular religion. Auntie Kath also talked to me a lot about modern literature and about religion, and once I discussed religion with a Devonshire dairy farmer, my landlord at the time, who solemnly assured me that he believed in the historical existence of Adam and Eve and who was as astonished to find that I did not believe in it as I was to find that he did.

Even after my emancipation from the wheelchair I had continued to read voraciously, borrowing from the Tooting Public Library books on a variety of subjects including, especially, literature, history, and philosophy. My pocket money did not stretch to buying books except for half a dozen volumes in the Thinker's Library series, published by the Rationalist Press Association, which were remarkably cheap. The volumes I bought included Samuel Butler's *The Fair Haven*, *Selected Works of Voltaire, including his celebrated poem on the Lisbon earthquake and 'The Questions of Zapata', and Gibbon on Christianity, being chapters XV and XVI of the great historian's History of the Decline and Fall of the Roman Empire*. In Torquay, however, though I continued to borrow books from the public library, as I had done in Barnstaple, once I had started work I was able to buy them. Among the first books I bought were *Selections from St Thomas Aquinas and The Little Flowers*, and *The Life of St Francis, both published in the Everyman's Library series*.

The life of St Francis, as it emerges from the pages of *The Little Flowers* and St Bonaventura's short biography, must have affected me quite deeply. At this time of my life, and perhaps for a long time afterwards, I was of an extremely impressionable nature, and like the crystal in the traditional Indian simile, which takes on the colour of whatever object is placed next to it, I readily took on the mood, the emotional colouring as it were, of whatever book I happened to be reading. Thus it was that when, one morning on my way to work, I was accosted by a beggar, I saw standing before me not a beggar but Christ himself, just as St Francis might have done, and at once gave him all the money I had on me.

With this dramatic experience my contact with Christianity, as mediated by the written word, came to an end, for the time being. I had started borrowing from the Torquay Public Library, or buying, books on Hinduism, on Islam, and on Theosophy. Among the books I borrowed were the two stout volumes of H.P. Blavatsky's *Isis Unveiled*, one of the foundational documents of the Theosophical movement, both of which I read through twice, from cover to cover, within a fortnight. What I would make of it if I were to read the work now, I do not know, but its effect on me was far-reaching in its consequences. The emotion I felt at the time is evident from what I wrote two decades later:

> Impressed, bewildered, thrilled, excited, stimulated as I was by their staggeringly immense wealth – their 'inexhaustible truckloads', as Maeterlinck called them – of information on every conceivable aspect of philosophy, comparative religion, occultism, mysticism, science, and a hundred other subjects, the realization which dawned most clearly upon me, and which by the time I had finished stood out with blinding obviousness in the very forefront of my consciousness, was the fact that I *was not a Christian* – that I never had been, and never would be – and that the whole structure of Christian doctrine was from beginning to end thoroughly repugnant to me. This realization gave me a sense of relief, of liberation as from some oppressive burden, which was so great that I wanted to sing and dance for joy. What I was, what I believed, I knew not, but what I was not and what I did not believe, that I knew with utter certainty, and this knowledge, merely negative though it was as yet, gave me a foretaste of that freedom which comes when all obstacles are removed, all barriers broken down, all limitations transcended.

I spent seven or eight months in Torquay. At the end of this period I returned to London, as I was feeling homesick. I had been away a year. For the next few months I did little except read books on my favourite subjects and write poetry, which I had been doing for some time. I borrowed books not only from the Tooting Public Library, as I had done before, but also from its counterpart in Streatham High Street, which had a better philosophy section. The only book on Christianity that I can recall reading at this time was Newman's *The Arians of the Fourth Century*, which I probably read as much for its literary style as for its contents.

This idyllic existence came to an end in November 1941, when I started working at County Hall. The fact that I now had a full-time job meant that I had less time for reading; but it also meant that since I was working I was earning, and since I was earning I had money with which to buy books. Soon I was spending much of my lunch hour, and most of Saturday afternoon, browsing in the bookshops of Charing Cross Road. In one of these I came across translations of the *Diamond Sūtra* and the *Sūtra of Wei Lang* (Hui Neng). These two books changed my life. Reading them I realized that I was a Buddhist, and always had been one. Though I continued to have contact with Christianity, at least from time to time, henceforth I was in contact with it *as a Buddhist*.

CHAPTER
TWO

THE BIBLE AS LITERATURE

FOR ME, 'THE BIBLE' MEANS THE ENGLISH BIBLE. More specifically, it means the Authorized Version of 1611, so called on account of its having been 'newly translated out of the original tongues' by command of King James I. For me, therefore, the Bible is primarily a literary work, or rather, a collection of such works, and is as much a part of English literature as Dryden's *Virgil*, Pope's *Homer*, or FitzGerald's *Omar Khayyám*.

The fact that for me the Bible is a literary work means that, for me, it cannot be the Word of God. Quite apart from the circumstance that I am a Buddhist, and do not believe in the existence of a personal God, the creator and ruler of the universe, the fact that the Bible is clearly the work of a number of writers, living at widely separate periods, and that it contains as many factual errors, contradictions, and interpolations, as any other body of ancient writings, makes it impossible for me to regard it as the work of an omniscient author who at different times has dictated it, as it were, to various human amanuenses.

I have never read the Bible straight through, from the Book of Genesis to the Book of Revelation, as some pious Christians do every year, but in the course of my life I have read most of it, and some parts I have read a number of times. When I was in my teens my favourite books were the Book of Job and the Song of Solomon, especially the former, which I read over and over again. I had the good fortune to possess a separate edition of these works which besides printing the text as poetry, as the Authorized Version of 1611 had done, also contained Blake's illustrations, which I have always admired no less than the Book of Job itself. According to modern scholarship the work was probably composed at the beginning of the fifth century BCE. The first two chapters are in prose, as is the last chapter. In between are fifty chapters of very fine, if sometimes repetitive, poetry. The poem revolves around a fundamental problem: why does the good man suffer? The ancient Jews believed that the good man did *not* suffer; only the wicked suffer. If a man fears God, and eschews evil, God will bless him with long life, offspring, and material wealth. Job is a good man, perfect and upright, and God had blessed him with seven sons and three daughters, and with seven thousand sheep, three thousand camels, five hundred yoke of oxen, five hundred she asses, and a very great household. But suppose God were to take all that away. Would Job not curse God?

The story begins in heaven. One day the sons of God come to present themselves before the Lord, and Satan also comes. He has been visiting the earth, and the Lord asks him if he has observed Job, a perfect and upright man, who fears God and eschews evil. Satan replies that he has indeed observed him. But Job has good reason to fear God, he says, for has not God always protected him and all his possessions? If the Lord were to deprive him of his possessions Job would curse him to his face. The Lord thereupon delivers all Job's possessions into the power of Satan, but not Job himself. On one and the same day, the Sabeans fall upon his oxen and his asses and take them away, the fire of God falls from heaven and burns up his sheep, the Caldeans carry away his camels, and a great wind comes from the desert and blows down the house in which his sons and daughters are feasting, killing them all. Yet despite his misfortunes Job does not curse God. 'Naked came I out of my mother's womb,' he says, 'naked shall I return thither: the Lord gave, and the Lord hath taken away, blessed be the Name of the Lord.' Satan therefore again presents himself before the Lord. This time the Lord delivers Job's body into his power, though not his life, whereupon Satan smites Job with boils, from the soles of his feet to the crown of his head. Taking a fragment of pottery with which to scrape himself, Job then sits down among ashes, where he is visited by his three friends, Eliphaz, Bildad, and Zophar, who have heard of his misfortunes and have come to comfort him. For seven days and seven nights they sit down with him on the ground, out of sympathy not saying a word. At last Job speaks, cursing the day he was born, and the poem proper begins:

> Let the day perish, wherein I was born,
> And the night in which it was said,
> There is a man-child conceived.
> Let that day be darkness,
> Let not God regard it from above,
> Neither let the light shine upon it.
> Let darkness and the shadow of death stain it,
> Let a cloud dwell upon it,
> Let the blackness of the day terrify it.
> As for that night, let darkness seize upon it,
> Let it not be joined unto the days of the year,
> Let it not come into the number of the months.
> Lo, let that night be solitary,
> Let no joyful voice come from therein.
> Let them curse it that curse the day,
> Who are ready to raise up their mourning.
> Let the stars of the twilight thereof be dark,
> Let it look for light, but have none,
> Neither let it see the dawning of the day:
> Because it shut not up the doors of my mother's womb,
> Nor hid sorrow from mine eyes.
> Why died I not from the womb?
> Why did I not give up the ghost when I came out of the belly?
> Why did the knees prevent me?
> Or why the breasts, that I should suck?
> For now should I have lien still and been quiet,
> I should have slept; then had I been at rest,
> With Kings and counsellors of the earth,
> Which built desolate places for themselves,
> Or with Princes that had gold,
> Who filled their houses with silver:
> Or as a hidden untimely birth, I had not been;

As infants which never saw light.
There the wicked cease from troubling:
And there the weary be at rest.[1]

When Job has concluded his speech, of which I have quoted rather more than half, Eliphaz replies to him at even greater length. In the words of the translators' marginal note, he 'reproveth Job for want of religion'. No one who is innocent ever perishes, he declares, as Job himself has formerly taught many; but now when he is being afflicted himself, he complains and questions God's justice. Instead of complaining, he should reflect on the greatness of God and be glad that God is punishing him, for in the long run this will benefit him greatly.

Job will have none of this. He has cause for complaint, he exclaims, and after reproving his friend for his unkindness he proceeds to give eloquent expression to his desire for death, a desire which, he says, is quite justified. Bildad then speaks. How much longer will he go on repeating the same thing, he impatiently asks Job. God deals with men according to their works, as history abundantly shows. He punishes the wicked, and Job's present plight is simply an example of his justice. Job acknowledges God's justice, but goes on to argue that although God can destroy both the perfect and the wicked, if he so wills, the fact that he has afflicted him does not mean that he is not innocent. He then expostulates with God, asking why he has afflicted him. God knows he is not wicked. Why, then, should he afflict him, the work of his hands. He has suffered enough, he tells God. All he now wants is a little ease before death. Zophar then joins in the discussion, reproving Job for insisting on his innocence, and emphasizing that God's wisdom is unfathomable. To this Job replies in a long speech, occupying three chapters, in the course of which he acknowledges God's omnipotence, reproves his friends for their partiality, and affirms his confidence in God. 'Though he slay me, yet will I trust in him', he says. Eliphaz now speaks for the second time, again

1 Quotations in this chapter are taken from *The Tudor Translations*, edited by W.E. Henley, published by David Nutt, London 1903.

reproving Job for insisting on his innocence and describing at length the unhappiness of the wicked.

By this time Job has lost patience with his friends. 'Miserable comforters are ye all', he tells them. But the debate continues nevertheless for sixteen more chapters, after which Job's three 'comforters' fall silent, 'because he is righteous in his own eyes'. Elihu, who so far has not been mentioned, now speaks. (His speech may be an interpolation.) He is a much younger man, and has not spoken before out of respect for his elders. He is angry with Job because he 'justifies' himself, and with Job's three friends because they have not been able to convince him. He himself succeeds no better, however. Though he speaks at length, he is able to add little to what the friends had already said, and Job does not bother to answer him.

We are now nine tenths of our way through the work and have reached its climax – the Lord's speech. The Lord's speech covers four chapters, and is interrupted only by Job's brief acknowledgement of his vileness. He does not tell Job why he has been afflicted. Instead, speaking 'out of the whirlwind', he overwhelms him with a declaration of his greatness and power, as manifested by the whole of creation, saying:

> Who is this that darkneth counsel
> By words without knowledge?
> Gird up now thy loins like a man;
> For I will demand of thee, and answer thou me.
> Where wast thou when I laid the foundations of the earth?
> Declare, if thou hast understanding.
> Who hath laid the measures thereof, if thou knowest?
> Or who hath stretched the line upon it?
> Whereupon are the foundations thereof fastened?
> Or who laid the corner stone thereof?
> When the morning stars sang together,
> And all the sons of God shouted for joy.
> Or who shut up the sea with doors,
> When it brake forth as if it had issued out of the womb?

> When I made the cloud the garment thereof,
> And thick darkness a swaddling band for it,
> And brake up for it my decreed place,
> And set bars and doors,
> And said, Hitherto shalt thou come, but no further:
> And here shall thy proud waves be stayed.

He goes on in this vein, at one point asking Job, with heavy sarcasm, if he knows where light and darkness dwell because he was born then, or because the number of his days is great. More rhetorical questions follow:

> Hast thou entered into the springs of the sea?
> Or hast thou walked in the search of the depth?
> Have the gates of death been opened unto thee?
> Or hast thou seen the doors of the shadow of death?
> Hast thou perceived the breadth of the earth?
> Declare if thou knowest it all.
> Where is the way where light dwelleth?
> And as for darkness, where is the place thereof?
> That thou shouldest take it to the bound thereof,
> And that thou shouldest know the paths to the house thereof.
> Knowest thou it, because thou wast then born?
> Or because the number of thy days is great?
> Hast thou entered into the treasures of the snow?
> Or hast thou seen the treasures of the hail,
> Which I have reserved against the time of trouble,
> Against the day of battle and war?
> By what way is the light parted?
> Which scattereth the East wind upon the earth.
> Who hath divided a water-course for the overflowing of waters?
> Or a way for the lightning of thunder,
> To cause it to rain on the earth, where no man is:
> On the wilderness wherein there is no man?
> To satisfy the desolate and waste ground,
> And to cause the bud of the tender herb to spring forth.
> Hath the rain a father?
> Or who hath begotten the drops of dew?

Out of whose womb came the ice?
And the hoary frost of heaven, who hath gendered it?
The waters are hid as with a stone,
And the face of the deep is frozen.

The Lord then directs Job's attention to the animal kingdom, asking him if he knows the ways of the hind, the wild asses, and the unicorn, and whether he is able to control them. Next, Job is asked about the horse, which the unknown author of the book of Job describes in a manner that shows he had a painter's eye for the beauties and splendours of the natural world:

Hast thou given the horse strength?
Hast thou clothed his neck with thunder?
Canst thou make him afraid as a grasshopper?
The glory of his nostrils is terrible.
He paweth in the valley, and rejoiceth in his strength:
He goeth on to meet the armed men.
He mocketh at fear, and is not affrighted:
Neither turneth he back from the sword.
The quiver ratleth against him,
The glittering spear and the shield.
He swalloweth the ground with fierceness and rage:
Neither believeth he that it is the sound of the trumpet.
He saith among the trumpets, Ha, ha:
And he smelleth the battle afar off,
The thunder of the captains, and the shouting.

Finally, after demanding of Job if he will disannul his judgement, or if he is in any way like him, he directs his attention first to Behemoth and then to Leviathan:

Behold now Behemoth which I made with thee,
He eateth grass as an ox.
Lo now, his strength is in his loins,
And his force is in the navel of his belly.
He moveth his tail like a Cedar:
The sinews of his stones are wrapt together.

His bones are as strong pieces of brass:
His bones are like bars of iron.
He is the chief of the ways of God:
He that made him, can make his sword to approach unto him.
Surely the mountains bring him forth food:
Where all the beasts of the field play.
He lieth under the shady trees,
In the covert of the reed, and fens.
The shady trees cover him with their shadow:
The willows of the brook compass him about.
Behold, he drinketh up a river, and hasteth not:
He trusteth that he can draw up Jordan into his mouth.
He taketh it with his eyes:
His nose pearceth through snares.

The description of Leviathan is much longer, and no less magnificent, and concludes:

He maketh the sea like a pot of ointment.
He maketh a path to shine after him;
One would think the deep to be hoary.
Upon earth there is not his like:
Who is made without fear.
He beholdeth all high things:
He is a king over all the children of pride.

The Lord's speech having come to an end, Job submits himself to God:

I have heard of thee by the hearing of the ear:
But now my eyes seeth thee.
Wherefore I abhor myself, and repent
In dust and ashes.

The story ends with the Lord telling Eliphaz, in the concluding prose chapter, that he is angry with him and his two friends for not having spoken rightly of God, as Job had done. They are to offer up seven bullocks and seven rams by way of penance and

Job is to pray for them. Job himself is accepted by the Lord, who gives him three new daughters and seven new sons, and double the number of sheep, camels, and yoke of oxen than he had before. Moreover, Job lives a hundred and forty years and sees his sons' sons, even to four generations.

The Book of Job has been described as the masterpiece of Hebrew literature, a judgement from which it is difficult to dissent. It is not a theodicy. It does not attempt to 'justify God's ways to men'. Indeed, it views any such attempt as presumptuous. Its God is not the God of love but the God of power – a power as manifest in the physical universe, from the starry heavens to the creatures of the earth, including man. As such he is well able to inflict suffering on man, but he cannot tell him why he does so. Though the Book of Job does not say so, man's questions must be answered by man himself.

The Song of Solomon is much shorter than the Book of Job, and is not nearly so great a work. But it contains some lovely poetry, the rhythms of which – in the Authorized Version – are much lighter than are those of the magnificent strophes of the Book of Job. Though the work is ascribed to King Solomon, it has no connection with him, and in its present form belongs to a much later period. It consists of a series of love poems – or wedding songs – which in one modern translation are distributed, quite plausibly, among the Bridegroom, the Bride, and the Chorus. I have always loved its celebration of the coming of Spring, when the lover – or Bridegroom – shows himself through the lattice, and says:

> Rise up, my Love, my fair one, and come away.
> For lo, the winter is past,
> The rain is over, and gone.
> The flowers appear on the earth,
> The time of the singing of birds is come,
> And the voice of the turtle is heard in our land.
> The fig tree putteth forth her green figs,
> And the vines with the tender grape
> Give a good smell.
> Arise, my Love, my fair one, and come away.

There is also a passage which itemizes the charms of the loved one in terms that modern taste is likely to find odd, even grotesque; such descriptions are not unusual in Elizabethan and Jacobean poetry:

> How beautiful are thy feet with shoes, O prince's daughter!
> The joints of thy thighs are like jewels,
> The work of the hands of a cunning workman.
> Thy navel is like a round goblet,
> Which wanteth not liquor:
> Thy belly is like an heap of wheat,
> Set about with lilies.
> Thy two breasts are like two young Roes
> That are twins.
> Thy neck is as a tower of ivory:
> Thine eyes like the fish pools in Heshbon, by the gate of
>   Bathrabbim:
> Thy nose is as the tower of Lebanon,
> Which looketh toward Damascus.
> Thine head upon thee is like Carmel,
> And the hair of thine head like purple,
> The king is held in the galleries.
> How fair, and how pleasant art thou,
> O Love, for delights!
> This thy stature is like to a palm tree,
> And thy breasts to clusters of grapes.

A more solemn note is struck in a short passage near the end of the work, where the lover says:

> Set me as a seal upon thine heart, as a seal upon thine arm:
> For love is strong as death,
> Jealousy is cruel as the grave:
> The coals thereof are coals of fire,
> Which hath a most vehement flame.
> Many waters cannot quench love,
> Neither can the floods drown it.

The Song of Solomon was accepted into the Jewish canon of scriptures only after its contents had been interpreted as an elaborate allegory of God's love for his chosen people, the Jews. When the books of the Old Testament became part of the Christian Bible, the Song of Songs continued to be treated as an allegory, this time as an allegory of Christ's love for the Church and the Church's love for Christ. Some of the Christian mystics, especially those of a more devotional type, continued this tradition of allegorical interpretation of the work, in whose erotic imagery they found a language for the expression of their devotional longings and spiritual experiences. St Bernard once delivered a series of impassioned sermons on the work, while its imagery informs some of the most beautiful poetry of St John of the Cross.

The Book of Job and the Song of Solomon both belong to a group of works known as the 'wisdom writings', as do the Book of Psalms, the Proverbs, and Ecclesiastes or the Preacher. They are called wisdom writings because Jewish tradition ascribes most of them to the proverbially wise King Solomon, and the wisdom of which they treat is of a worldly, prudential kind that does not exclude an element of theistic piety. The Psalms have never appealed to me, but I have dipped into Proverbs from time to time and have come across such maxims as 'whoso loveth instruction, loveth knowledge; But he that hateth reproof, is brutish', and 'A soft answer turneth away wrath; but grievous words stir up anger', both of which have their parallels in the much more ancient wisdom literature of Babylon and Egypt. I have also enjoyed, in the admonition to the sluggard, the delightful vignette of the busy ant:

> Go to the Ant, thou sluggard,
> Consider her ways, and be wise.
> Which have no guide,
> Overseer, or ruler,
> Provideth her meat in the Summer,
> And gathereth her food in the harvest.
> How long wilt thou sleep, O sluggard?
> When wilt thou arise out of thy sleep?

Yet a little sleep, a little slumber,
A little folding of the hands to sleep.
So shall thy poverty come as one that travaileth,
And thy want as an armed man.

I have also appreciated the realistic description, from the unknown author's personal observation, of what the marginal note
bluntly calls 'the cunning of a whore':

For at the window of my house
I looked through my casement,
And beheld among the simple ones,
I discerned among the youths,
A young man void of understanding,
Passing through the street near her corner,
And he went the way to her house,
In the twilight in the evening,
In the black and dark night:
And behold, there met him a woman,
With the attire of an harlot, and subtle of heart.
(She is loud and stubborn,
Her feet abide not in her house:
Now is she without, now in the streets,
And lieth in wait at every corner.)
So she caught him, and kissed him,
And with an impudent face, said unto him,
I have peace offerings with me:
This day have I paid my vows.
Therefore came I forth to meet thee,
Diligently to seek thy face, and I have found thee.
I have decked my bed with coverings of tapestry,
With carved works, with fine linen of Egypt.
I have perfumed my bed
With myrrh, aloes, and cinnamon.
Come, let us take our fill of love until the morning,
Let us solace our selves with loves.
For the good-man is not at home,
He is gone a long journey.

He hath taken a bag of money with him,
And will come home at the day appointed.
With much fair speech she caused him to yield,
With the flattering of her lips she forced him.
He goeth after her straightway,
As an ox goeth to the slaughter,
Or as a fool to the correction of the stocks,
Till a dart strike through his liver,
As a bird hasteth to the snare,
And knoweth not that it is for his life.

My least favourite books of the Bible are the so-called historical books of the Old Testament, such as the Book of Judges, and 1 and 2 Samuel, which are not genuine histories but a mixture of history, folklore, legend, and myth. They contain some good stories, some of which are as familiar to me from certain Renaissance paintings as they are from the pages of the Bible. But the historical books also contain much that I find abhorrent, so that I can well understand why Aldous Huxley should have referred to the Old Testament as 'this savage Bronze Age literature'. For example, in I Samuel the Lord commands King Saul, through the prophet Samuel, to destroy the Amalekites, saying:

Now go and smite Amalek, and utterly destroy all that they have, and spare them not; but slay both man and woman, infant and suckling, ox and sheep, camel and ass.

Since for orthodox Christians the Bible, including the historical books, is the Word of God, passages like this one have enabled them to conduct crusades and pogroms with a clear conscience.

For me, then, the Bible is literature, and it is as literature that I enjoy it. That it is not the Word of God does not mean that, for me, it is not inspired. Some parts of it, at least, are inspired in much the same way that some of my favourite poets are inspired, and in my book that is no small praise.

Chapter

Three

The Church

WHEN I WAS A SMALL BOY, growing up in South London, I was reminded, every year, of the Catholic conspiracy to blow up James I and his parliament on 5 November 1605. 'Please to remember the fifth of November, gunpowder, treason, and plot', we chanted at school on the anniversary of that day; and in the evening, as soon as it was dark, we burnt an effigy – a 'guy' – of Guy Fawkes on a bonfire in our back yards and let off fireworks.

The Gunpowder Plot must have left deep traces in the English folk memory for us to be still celebrating Guy Fawkes Day or Bonfire Night, as it was also called, more than three hundred years after the event. It was as though we had always known about the Plot and about how Guy Fawkes was surprised, in the vaults below the Palace of Westminster, with barrels of gunpowder and a lighted torch. There were other traces, left by earlier events in English history in which Catholics, or the Roman Catholic Church, had played a sinister part. There was the Spanish Armada of 1588, which Philip II of Spain had launched with the object of dethroning Elizabeth, installing her Catholic cousin Mary, Queen of Scots in her place, and with the help of the Inquisition returning England to the Catholic fold. We knew about the great Armada, and about how it had been defeated by Drake and the elements, not so much from our history lessons as from stories in the various boys' papers that were set in that period.

Later, I learned about the Ridolfi Plot, the aim of which was to assassinate Elizabeth, place Mary on the throne, bring about a general uprising of Catholics against the government, and restore

Catholicism as the religion of the land. The plot had been sanctioned, in effect, by Pope Pius V's bull of 1570, in which he denounced Elizabeth as a heretic, excommunicated her, and absolved her subjects from all obedience to her. A subsequent directive from the papal Secretary of State decreed that if any English gentleman were to undertake the 'glorious work' of assassinating Queen Elizabeth it would not be regarded as a sin.

In the previous reign, that of Elizabeth's Catholic half-sister Mary I, there had taken place an event that probably left even deeper traces in the English folk memory than the Gunpowder Plot. This was the burning at the stake, as heretics, of nearly three hundred Protestants of both sexes and all ages. Among the victims were Bishops Ridley and Latimer, and Archbishop Cranmer, who met their deaths in Oxford in 1555 and 1556, near the spot on which a memorial to them, erected in 1839, now stands. Latimer's last words to his colleague Ridley were, 'Be of good cheer, Master Ridley, for I trust that this day we will light such a candle in England as by God's grace shall never be put out.'

I do not remember when I first read about the Ridolfi Plot or about the burning of Protestants in the reign of Mary I – 'Bloody Mary', as she came to be called – but I retain a distinct visual impression of two illustrations I saw, illustrations connected with two of the most horrifying episodes in European religious history. I came upon the first of these while still confined to bed, and I came upon it in the *Children's Encyclopedia*. It depicted a scene in the English embassy at the time of the Massacre of St Bartholomew's Eve, when in 1572, in the course of a single week, 25,000 Huguenots – French Protestants – were slaughtered in Paris and elsewhere in the country on the orders of the French king, Charles IX. In the illustration seven or eight men are gathered in front of a large window, their backs to the viewer. They are observing the carnage going on outside. To the right, an older man stands with hands clasped behind his back and head bowed, deep in thought. In the foreground, one woman bends solicitously over another, whose head is buried in the lap of a third woman.

The second illustration occupied the front cover of a booklet I bought in Westminster Cathedral, on the occasion when my mother and I visited it with my Auntie Kate. The booklet was about the Spanish Inquisition, and the illustration depicted a single figure. He is carrying a lighted taper, and on his head there is a kind of dunce's cap inscribed with various symbols. His posture is extremely dejected. Apparently he is a reclaimed heretic doing public penance for his sins.

The two illustrations must have affected me deeply for me to have retained visual images of them for so long. I must have felt the horror, the grief, and the distress of those people in the English embassy and have shared the dejection of the penitent. I certainly have a clear recollection of what I thought and felt when I read the booklet I had bought. The author did not seek to deny that the Inquisition had burnt people at the stake, which he could hardly have done without blushing, but he sought to excuse the Inquisition, to an extent, by maintaining that the total number of persons burnt had been greatly exaggerated by Protestant historians. It was not true, as they alleged, that altogether 80,000 persons had been burnt. It was only 30,000. To me this quibbling over numbers was shockingly beside the point. It was horrible that *anyone* should be burnt at the stake. It was horrible that Catholics should kill Protestants and that such killing should have the sanction, even the blessing, of the pope, the head of the Roman Catholic Church. Later I discovered that the reigning pope had struck a medal commemorating the Massacre of St Bartholomew's Eve, and that it was one of his predecessors who, in 1231 CE, had established the Inquisition, or Holy Office, as it was later styled, to suppress heresy.

My feelings in this connection led me, in the next few years, to take an interest in the history of the Church. For me, 'the Church' means the Roman Catholic Church. This is not because I believe the Roman Catholic Church to have a monopoly of Christian faith or Christian virtue, but because I am a European, and from 313 CE, when Constantine formally recognized Christianity as one of the religions legally permitted within the Roman Empire, to 31 October 1517, when Martin Luther nailed his 95 theses to the door of a church in Wittenberg, the history of Europe and the history of the Roman Catholic Church have been virtually inseparable. I did not study the subject systematically, but picked up knowledge about it in the course of my general reading, which at this time included John Addington Symonds' *The Renaissance in Italy*, Mandell Creighton's *History of the Papacy*, and biographies of Elizabeth I and Savonarola (all borrowed from the Tooting Public Library). I also learned something of the reign of Henry VIII, father of Mary I and Elizabeth I, in whose reign there took place the greatest upheaval in the religio-political history of England since the arrival of St Augustine on these shores in 597 CE.

Between 1532 and 1539, exasperated by the continued reluctance of Clement VII to grant him a divorce from Catherine of Aragon, who had failed to produce a male heir to the throne, Henry rejected the authority of the pope, abolished annates to Rome, dissolved the monasteries, declared himself Head of the Church in England, and married Anne Boleyn, the mother of the future Queen Elizabeth. This did not mean that from being Roman Catholic England became Protestant all at once. Henry himself was theologically conservative, and more than one 'heretic' was burnt at the stake in his reign. Mary's four-year reign saw a violent swing from the Protestantism of her brother Edward VI, Henry's immediate successor, back to the Roman Catholic Church, the pope's supremacy being restored and Protestants persecuted. It was only during the long reign of Elizabeth, with her decided preference for the via media, that Protestantism in its moderate Anglican form became the predominant – and official – religion of the English people.

But why was it necessary for Henry VIII to ask the Pope, more than a thousand miles away in Rome, to grant him a divorce from Catherine of Aragon? And why was the Pope so reluctant to accede to his request? The short answer to the first question, I discovered, was that marriage and divorce, like so much else at the time, were matters that came within the jurisdiction of the Church, the supreme head of which was the Pope; to the second,

that as ruler of the States of the Church – the vast stretch of territory that occupied much of central Italy – the Pope was subject to
political and military pressure from other European rulers, especially, at that time, from the Holy Roman emperor, Charles V,
whose troops had sacked Rome in 1527 and who for reasons both
personal and political did not want Henry to get his divorce. But
how had the pope – how had the papacy – come to possess so
much power, both spiritual and temporal? *That* was the question
that now confronted me.

But by the time I reached this point Buddhism had begun to
occupy the forefront of my consciousness, so that it was only
much later, after my return to England after spending twenty
years in the East that, conscious I was teaching the Dharma in a
country still predominantly Christian, I picked up the threads of
my old studies and gave some attention to Christianity, including
the Church. Meanwhile, popes had come and popes had gone,
and John XXIII and his Vatican Council had done their work.
Much that hitherto had been deemed an essential part of the
building had been dismantled, so that the nature of the Church's
structure could now be more clearly discerned. Basically, the
Roman Catholic Church was – or at least had been, until recently
– a spiritual-cum-temporal kingdom – Christendom – of which
the pope was king possessing both spiritual and temporal power.

It was not always so. Believing that Christ would soon return and
establish his kingdom, the little Christian church in Rome, with
its bishop, refused to take part in the civil and military life of the
Roman state. Its members were accordingly proscribed and
persecuted by the authorities and regarded as criminals by the
rest of society. Being a Christian meant being ready to face death
at any time. In 313 CE all this changed. Constantine, the first Christian emperor of Rome, in that year recognized Christianity as one
of the religions permitted within the Roman empire. Nor was this
all. The following year he gave the then bishop of the Christian
church in Rome, Silvester I, one of the imperial palaces to live in,
an enormous amount of money, and much real estate, this

becoming the occasion, a thousand years later, of Dante's sorrowful reproach, as translated by Milton:

> Ah Constantine, of how much ill was cause
> Not thy conversion, but those rich domains
> That the first wealthy pope received of thee.

The 'ill' consisted in the fact that the patronage of Constantine transformed the bishop of the Christian church in Rome into 'the Pope', a temporal as well as a spiritual ruler, and his church into the Roman Catholic Church. Before long the Church had its own government (the hierarchy), its own legal system (canon law), its own court (the hated 'ecclesiastical court' of English history), its own fortresses and prisons, and eventually its own army.

Silvester's spiritual power was not bestowed on him by Constantine. It resided in the fact that as Bishop of Rome he was the successor of the Apostle Peter, the first bishop, to whom Christ had said, 'Thou art Peter, and on this rock I will build my church; and the gates of hell shall not prevail against it. And I will give unto thee the keys of the kingdom of heaven; and whatsoever thou shalt bind on earth shall be bound in heaven: and whatsoever thou shalt loose on earth shall be loosed in heaven' (Matthew 16:18–19). It was by virtue of the spiritual power entrusted by Christ to St Peter, and possessed by all Peter's successors as Bishop of Rome, that the Pope could excommunicate individuals and communities, and place whole kingdoms under an interdict. Innocent III excommunicated King John and placed England under an interdict (1208 CE) when John resisted his attempts to encroach upon the traditional right of the English crown in episcopal elections. Excommunication not only meant being expelled from the visible Church on earth; by virtue of Christ's promise to Peter it also meant being excluded from heaven. Under an interdict the clergy were prohibited from administering the sacraments and the dead could not be buried in consecrated ground. In the Ages of Faith, when men believed that 'outside the Church there is no salvation', excommunication and interdict were formidable weapons, and the popes did not hesitate to employ them in support of their increasingly grandiose claims, whether spiritual or temporal. They were the means by which recalcitrant princes could be brought to heel, as King John eventually was.

In Shakespeare's *King John* there is a scene in which the king surrenders his crown to Cardinal Pandulph, 'the holy legate of the pope', who hands it back to him in token of the fact that, as the legate says, John now holds his royal authority 'of the pope', meaning that John is now the pope's vassal. A few years ago I attended a performance of *King John* at Stratford-upon-Avon, Shakespeare's birthplace, and was greatly struck by the way in which this scene was presented. Only Pandulph and the king were on stage. Pandulph, in his scarlet robes, was enthroned aloft, his head almost touching the ceiling, while John crouched below him in a posture of abject surrender. At this point in the production I thought I felt a kind of frisson run through the audience, as if some members of it had been put in mind of the fact that, eight hundred years after King John, the country might again have to give up its sovereignty, this time not to Rome but to Brussels. When *King John* was first performed, sometime between 1591 and 1598, much more then a frisson must have passed through the audience. They must have remembered, with a surge of patriotic pride, the defeat of the Spanish Armada and the failure of Philip II's attempt to bring England back into the Roman Catholic Church by force of arms.

Be that as it may, the scene from *King John*, as I saw it acted that evening, was a perfect representation of the blatant triumphalism of the medieval papacy, whose spiritual-cum-temporal power was at its height during the reign of Innocent III, before it was weakened by the Great Schism, when two, even three, rival popes cursed and excommunicated each other. Innocent III (1198–1216) is in the line of Leo I, Gregory I, and Nicolas I, all of whom are styled 'the Great' because they had a 'high' conception of the pope's prerogatives and sought – with varying degrees of success – to act in accordance with it. Leo I (440–461) laid down the doctrine that the bishops depended for the exercise of their jurisdiction on the pope, who alone possessed the plenitude of power. Gregory I (590–604) decreed that the pope alone had the right to depose emperors and kings; that the pope could absolve subjects from their oaths of loyalty; and that the pope could be judged by no one. Nicolas I (858–867) claimed the right to legislate for the whole of Christendom. In his view the pope was the supreme judge, by whom all major disputes were to be judged, and who could accept appeals from lesser courts.

These popes, more than any of the others, determined the basic mind-set of the Roman Catholic Church for centuries to come. It was a mind-set that was legalistic, intolerant, and authoritarian, and one that above all was bent on its own aggrandisement in the name of Christ. As late as 1864, when the papacy was about to lose what was left of the papal states, the then pope, Pius IX, condemned as erroneous the opinion that 'the Church has not the power of using force, nor has she any temporal power, direct or indirect'.

When the Devil tempted him in the wilderness, offering to give him 'all the kingdoms of the world, and the glory of them', if he would fall down and worship him, Jesus had said 'Get thee hence, Satan' (Matthew 4:8–10). Three hundred years later, when the Devil appeared again, in the benign form of the emperor Constantine, Silvester I did not treat him so rudely. He accepted the palace, the money, and the civil jurisdiction that were offered him, thus in effect falling down and worshipping the Devil.

The pope, now a ruler among rulers, used his temporal power as ruler of the papal states in the interests of his spiritual authority, and his spiritual power as Bishop of Rome, the successor of St Peter, in the interests of his – and the Church's – worldly power and prestige. Before long the two powers, and the two sets of interests, were virtually indistinguishable, and the Church became a spiritual-cum-temporal kingdom ruled by a pope-king who for a time was the most important ruler in Europe. 'Power tends to corrupt', wrote Lord Acton, historian and Roman Catholic, 'and absolute power corrupts absolutely'. The papacy never quite possessed absolute power, though it strove to achieve it, but the corruption nevertheless was spectacular. I was therefore not surprised, especially after I had read about the Renaissance popes, to learn that there were Protestants who identified the papacy with the Great Whore seen by St John the Divine in the Book of Revelation:

> And I saw a woman sit upon a scarlet coloured beast, full of names of blasphemy, having seven heads and ten horns. And the woman was arrayed in purple and scarlet colour, and decked with gold and precious stones and pearls, having a golden cup in her hand full of abominations and filthiness of her fornication: And on her forehead was a name written, MYSTERY, BABYLON THE GREAT, THE MOTHER OF HARLOTS AND ABOMINATIONS OF THE EARTH. And I saw the woman drunken with the blood of the saints, and with the blood of the martyrs of Jesus.[2]

For those who saw the papacy as the Great Whore, the blood with which the woman was drunk was the blood of the Protestant martyrs, like those who had been burnt at the stake in the reign of Mary I, or who had died in the Massacre of St Bartholomew's Eve.

That the Church was corrupt, inasmuch as it was based on power, did not mean that something of its original spirit did not survive within its massive structures. I am well aware that in every generation there were Catholics who led honourable and blameless lives, though the fact that they were members of the Church meant that they helped support, even if they did not directly contribute to, the general corruption. In recent times this has been much less the case than it was formerly, there now being much less of the Church to support, so to speak, even in countries where the population is largely Catholic. Since 1870, when the papacy was shorn of its temporal power, and especially since Vatican II, papal authority has weighed less heavily on clergy

2 Revelation 17:3–6

and laity alike than at any time in the Church's history. Interdicts are unknown, while the formal excommunication of Marcel Lefebvre in 1988 for the unauthorized ordination of priests – the first excommunication within the Church for more than a hundred years – was so exceptional as to be front page news.

One of the consequences of the Church's updating, as it has been called, is that Catholics are now free to enter into dialogue with the followers of other faiths, and even to learn about those faiths. In the course of the last fifty years, therefore, I have been able not only to read about the Church but also to have personal contact, as a Buddhist, with some of its more open-minded members. During my time in India most of the Christians I got to know were missionaries. Kalimpong, a hill station in the foothills of the eastern Himalayas, where I lived for fourteen years, was particularly rich in missionaries. There were the Scottish Presbyterians, who did their best to ignore me, the friendly American Seventh Day Adventists who invited me to lunch, and the two 'missionary girls' fresh from Bible college in England, who after their failure to convert me regarded me, with evident horror, as one of the irretrievably lost. There were also the loners, such as the saintly American member of the Cowley Fathers, an Anglican religious order, who loved lepers and scandalized his fellow missionaries by refusing to convert anyone, and the bumptious, red-bearded Scottish evangelist who belonged to no Christian body and who 'took his orders direct from God'. And there were the Roman Catholics.

The Catholics were the mainly Swiss priests and brothers at St Augustine's Priory and the nuns, some of them Indian, at St Philomena's Convent nearby. The former conducted a boarding school for boys, the latter a boarding school for girls. Each had built their own church. The priests and brothers had constructed theirs on the model of a Tibetan gompa, while the nuns had opted for something vaguely Gothic, with stained glass windows. Some of the brothers got into the habit of visiting me, as the rented building in which I was then living was situated half way between the priory and the bazaar, and it was easy for them to drop in on their way to market. I returned their visits, and in this way got to know some of them quite well. I lent them books on Buddhism and borrowed Christian classics from the Priory library, and we had long and interesting discussions on Buddhism, comparative religion, and mysticism. This friendly contact, which took place in the early 1950s, did not continue for more than two or three months. The brothers suddenly stopped coming to see me, and when I happened to meet them on the road they seemed embarrassed. Much later I learned that someone in authority had forbidden them to have anything more to do with me.

A year or two later I met a Roman Catholic of a very different kind from whoever it was had told the Augustinian brothers that they were to stop seeing me. This was a little gnome-like, bright-eyed French priest called Father Monchanin, one of the founders of the first 'Christian ashrams' in India, and thus a forerunner of the better known Father Bede Griffiths, whose autobiography, *The Golden String*, I read some years later. I met Father Monchanin not in Kalimpong but in Bangalore, at the Indian Institute of Culture, where for two hours or more we discussed Buddhism, especially the Madhyamikavada, Vedanta, and comparative mysticism. I would have liked to see more of Father Monchanin, but our paths did not cross again, though we exchanged a few letters, and not many years after our meeting he died.

At about the same time I made the acquaintance of two other Catholic priests, with one of whom I was to be in fairly regular contact for the rest of my time in India. I met both of them in Bombay, at the home of my Parsee friend Dinshaw Mehta, founder of the Society of Servants of God, with whom I often stayed when I was lecturing in that cosmopolitan city. Father Mascarenhas, a Goanese by birth, was a large, cheerful, communicative man in his mid-fifties with an enormous paunch that threatened to burst the buttons on his tightly stretched white soutane. A very learned man, the master of many languages, his views on Indian Catholicism, or rather, on Catholicism in India, were very much in accord with Father Monchanin's. He believed that the Church had to become culturally much more Indian. In particular, he believed that just as, in Europe, Catholic theology, in the person of St Thomas Aquinas, had absorbed and Christianized the philosophy of Aristotle, so in India it had to absorb and Christianize the philosophy of Śaṅkara, and since I had studied the works of the great exponent of Advaita Vedanta we had some interesting discussions. Father Mascarhenas also believed that the Three Magi who, in the Gospel According to St Matthew, present the infant Jesus with gold, frankincense, and myrrh, all came from Western India, possibly from Goa.

Not surprisingly, he was often in trouble with his ecclesiastical superiors for his views on the Indianization of the Church, and more than once had to appear before the Archbishop to receive a warning or a reprimand. For a period he had even been suspended from the exercise of his priestly functions, though for precisely what offence he did not say. All this was as water off a duck's back, however, and among his non-Christian friends, at least, he continued to air his unorthodox views, as well as to denounce what he called 'the Roman racket' in unsparing terms. Once he told me that he hated Christmas. He hated it because it was in the week before Christmas Day that many Bombay Catholics made their annual confession, and he was obliged to sit for hours on end listening to the same dreary catalogue of petty sins until he felt thoroughly nauseated. Later on, Father Mascarhenas may have had sins of his own to confess. The last time I had news of him, on a return visit to India, he had moved to Poona and was living with a woman.

The other priest I met only once. I do not remember his name, but I well remember his story. We met at the suggestion of my Theosophist friend Sophia Wadia, editor of the *Aryan Path*, who told me that the priest was in a state of great mental distress and might, she thought, find it helpful to talk to me. He came accompanied by an armed bodyguard in the form of two senior police officers, who stationed themselves in the hallway while we talked privately in my room. He was an ex-Jesuit, he explained, and until recently he had been professor of philosophy at a Catholic college near Bangalore. In his classes he had made it clear that certain truths the Church regarded as beyond doubt were, in fact, open to question, at least from the standpoint of philosophy, and could be freely discussed. For this he had got into serious trouble, both with the college authorities and with his Jesuit superiors, and in the end he had decided to leave both the Jesuit order and the Church. At one point he had had an interview with the head of the order in India, who told him that if he agreed to stay in the order and in the Church and to keep his ideas to himself he could have unlimited credit at his wine merchant and unlimited credit with his tailor. (I noticed that my visitor was elegantly dressed in sober black.) He had not agreed. Instead, he had resigned from the Jesuit order and made it known that he no longer considered himself a member of the Catholic Church. During the next few weeks he received more than 1,800 abusive and threatening letters (he told me the exact figure), many of them obscene, and some of them from distant parts of India. One night a group of men, in order to discredit him, had tried to introduce a prostitute into the cottage in which he had taken refuge. In desperation he had fled to Bombay, where Sophia Wadia and other influential friends had secured for him the protection of the police. He was evidently a refined, cultured, and sensitive person and I could see that the experiences he had undergone had left him badly shaken. What I said to him I do not remember. Perhaps all he needed at that time was a sympathetic ear. Nor do I know what happened to him afterwards, though on subsequent visits to Bombay I enquired after him.

'So the Church has been up to its old tricks,' I reflected after my visitor and his bodyguard had left. The Church had been up to its old tricks elsewhere in India too, as I was well aware. Recently one of the Jesuit fathers of North Point, the Catholic boys' college in Darjeeling, had gone to the Deputy Commissioner, the seniormost government officer in that part of West Bengal, and reported that I was a communist spy, at the same time suggesting that in the interest of national security I should be expelled from the Darjeeling district in which Kalimpong was located. Fortunately I knew the Deputy Commissioner and his wife and the next time we happened to meet he told me about the incident. 'I know very well why he reported you,' he added, 'you have nothing to worry about.'

The Church was up to its old tricks not only in India but also in South Vietnam. Like its immediate neighbours, Laos and Cambodia, Vietnam was a Buddhist country, though it did not, as they did, follow the Theravada, but the Mahayana in its Chinese form, with a mixture of Ch'an and Pure Land Buddhism predominating. In the seventeenth century French Catholics started missions, and it was not long before the Flag followed the Cross. Between 1858 and 1884 France conquered Vietnam, and with Cambodia and Laos it became part of the French colonial possession of Indo-China. After the Second World War, when Vietnam was occupied by the Japanese, France tried to regain control of the territory, being finally defeated at Dien Bien Phu only after eight years of bitter fighting. At the 1954 Geneva Conference the country was divided into communist North Vietnam, led by Ho Chi Minh, with its capital at Hanoi, and pro-Western South Vietnam, led by Ngo Dinh Diem, with its capital at Saigon.

President Diem was a Roman Catholic, as was his younger brother Ngo Dinh Nhu, whom he made his personal adviser and put in charge of Intelligence and the Secret Police. His elder brother Ngo Dinh Thuc was Roman Catholic Archbishop of Hue, while his sister-in-law Mme Nhu, described by her American admirer Clare Booth Luce as 'a militant Catholic', led the paramilitary women's organization. It was therefore not surprising that under the Diem regime, as under French colonial rule, the Catholic minority should have been supported and encouraged while the less organized Buddhist majority should have been discriminated against, suppressed, and finally systematically persecuted.

Things came to a head when on 6 May 1963 the President issued an order prohibiting the Buddhists of Hue from flying the Buddhist flag on the Buddha's birthday two days later, even though a few days earlier, on the occasion of a Catholic festival, the Vatican flag had been flown all over the city. On 8 May, their leaders having failed to get the order rescinded, the Buddhists of Hue protested against the ban by going in procession from Tu Dam Pagoda to the Hue Radio Station. There government troops broke up the procession with tear gas, then fired on the crowd. Twelve people were killed and more than fifty wounded. The Buddhist clergy and laity of South Vietnam then presented the Government with five requests, namely: (1) that the Government rescind the order prohibiting the flying of the Buddhist flag; (2) that Buddhism benefit from the same special treatment granted to the Roman Catholic missions; (3) that the Government stop arresting and terrorizing the Buddhists; (4) that the Buddhist clergy and laymen be free to practise their faith and to spread it; and (5) that the Government pay equitable compensation for the people killed and punish those responsible in a fitting manner.

These requests formed part of a manifesto, the concluding sentence of which read, 'We all are ready to sacrifice ourselves until these reasonable requests are granted.' Events soon showed Diem and the other members of the Catholic oligarchy that the Buddhists meant what they said. On 11 June a 67-year-old monk burnt himself to death in a crowded Saigon thoroughfare in protest against the government's persecution of the Buddhists. The monk, Thich Quong Duc, struck a match after his saffron robes were drenched with petrol, and sat motionless in the meditation posture while the flames enveloped him. Several hundred monks and nuns sat in a circle round the blazing body, chanting and weeping.

I was still living in India at the time and well remember the shock waves that went round the Buddhist world, as well as round India and the West, as reports of the self-immolation – and pictures of the burning monk – appeared in the newspapers. Only Vietnam's Roman Catholic oligarchy remained unmoved. 'If any more monks want to barbecue themselves,' Mme Nhu told reporters, 'I'll be happy to provide the petrol and a match.' More monks did want to 'barbecue' themselves, and in the course of the next few months, as the Diem government declared martial law and a state of siege, desecrated and destroyed major pagodas throughout South Vietnam, arrested and imprisoned thousands of monks and nuns, and held demonstrating students in concentration camps, eight more monks and one nun followed Thich Quong Duc's heroic example.

On 1 November the Diem government was overthrown by a long-expected *coup d'état* in which both the president and his younger brother were killed. Mme Nhu was then on the lecture tour in the United States, where she assured university audiences that there was no religious persecution in South Vietnam and that Vietnamese Buddhist monks were Communists in disguise. On being told of the *coup d'état* she angrily accused the United States government and the CIA of being behind it. This was in fact quite true, for Washington had become convinced that by persecuting the Buddhists Diem was undermining South Vietnam's – and the United States' – fight against Communism.

After my return to England in 1964 I was too busy teaching Buddhism and, eventually, starting a new Buddhist movement, to have much time for personal contact with Christians, whether Catholic or Protestant. I did, however, find time to read about Christianity. Besides taking up the thread of my old studies, as I have already related, I read several scholarly volumes on the Eastern Orthodox Church as well as a few works of popular theology. The most interesting of the latter was the best-selling *Honest to God* by John A. T. Robinson, then Bishop of Woolwich. It was of interest to me principally on account of the Bishop's apparent belief that theism was finished, a view that to my mind pointed in the direction of non-theistic religion, even in the direction of non-theistic Christianity, and thus to a possible overlap between Christianity and Buddhism, of which the Bishop seemed not to have heard. I therefore gave my usual Buddhist and quasi-Buddhist audience a lecture on 'Buddhism and the Bishop of Woolwich'. A member of the audience sent a tape-recording of the lecture to the Bishop, who eventually expressed a desire to meet me. We met at his house (bishops no longer lived in palaces), where we had a long and interesting, though not very deep, discussion in which, Dr Robinson being an Anglican bishop, his wife also joined.

For many years after this encounter I had no contact with Christians, so far as I remember, other than at the rather unexciting interfaith gatherings that I was occasionally prevailed upon to attend. After handing on my responsibilities as founder of the new Buddhist movement, which I did in the year 2000, at the age of 75, it occurred to me that I now had time to revisit the interfaith scene. I did this in Birmingham, where I was then living, and where I still live. At meetings of the Birmingham Council of Faiths I met Hindus, Muslims, Sikhs, Parsees, followers of the Baha'i faith, Roman Catholics, Protestants, and Jews, as well as fellow Buddhists following traditions other than my own.

Strange to relate, it was the Roman Catholics who seemed most interested in following up the contacts we had made. Thus I was invited to Oscott College, where I gave a talk on the Buddhist scriptures, was shown Cardinal Newman's rooms at the Birmingham Oratory, which he had founded, attended a mass celebrated by the new Archbishop of Birmingham, whom afterwards I met several times, and attended a reception given by the archdiocese to the Cardinal Archbishop of Westminster, whom I also met. I even started receiving each year on the anniversary of the Buddha's attainment of Supreme Enlightenment, a friendly message from the Vatican.

What had happened? Had the Roman Catholic Church experienced a change of heart? Did Roman Catholics no longer have to believe that there was no salvation outside the Church? And what of the past? Did the Church realize that it had been morally wrong for it to preach crusades and condemn heretics to death, and was it now trying to make amends? Or was the Catholic Church's present friendly attitude towards non-Catholics due to the fact that it no longer had any temporal power and that, in Britain at least, Catholics had been in a minority for several centuries, and therefore were more or less obliged to be friendly?

These were the sort of questions I wanted to ask my new friends, but before I knew them well enough to be able to ask them without giving offence I was struck down by chronic illness and the questions have remained, for the time being at least, unanswered.

Chapter
four

The Apostles' Creed

THOUGH I WAS BORN INTO A CHURCH OF ENGLAND FAMILY and
baptized in the parish church, I did not attend another Anglican
service until I was fourteen. This was when, as an evacuee in
Torquay, I attended, for a few Sundays, the church at which the
clergyman with whom I had been billeted officiated. It must have
been the morning service that I attended, for at one point I found
myself reciting, with the rest of the congregation, 'I believe in
God, the Father Almighty, Maker of heaven and earth: And in
Jesus Christ his only Son our Lord' – and so on through the other
clauses of what I subsequently learned was the Apostles' Creed. I
did not give much thought to what I was reciting but I remember
that when we came to the words 'he descended into hell' the
organ, which had been accompanying our recitation, sounded a
particularly deep and solemn note that vibrated through the little
church.

A creed has been defined as 'a form of words in which the articles
of faith are comprised' and the Apostles' Creed was the oldest of
the three creeds officially authorized by the Western Church, the
two others being the Nicene Creed and the Athanasian Creed. It
was used in the daily offices of the Roman Catholic and Anglican
churches, and in the services of several leading Protestant
churches. The Eastern Orthodox Church had its own versions of
the Apostles' Creed, and it did not regard the Athanasian Creed
as authoritative. Besides featuring in the Church of England's
morning service the Apostles' Creed also featured in its baptismal
service, and must have been recited by the congregation at my
own baptism as an infant.

Although infant baptism was practised in the Early Church, in the case of adults the candidate was interrogated before the ceremony, being asked 'Do you believe in God, the Father Almighty, Maker of heaven and earth?' and so on, and having to answer 'I do' as each clause was put to him in this manner in order to be accepted. In the Roman Catholic and Anglican churches the Apostles' Creed therefore has come to be known as 'the baptismal creed'. It is belief in the articles of faith comprised in this particular form of words that made one, in the Western Church at least, a Christian in the traditional sense. Hence if I want to know what Christians traditionally believe, and if, moreover, I want to find out to what extent my own beliefs, as a Buddhist, are in agreement with theirs, I would have to take a look at the Apostles' Creed.

Before I can take that look, however, I must clear up a possible confusion. It is a confusion of the kind that is likely to arise when the Inquisition, for example, is discussed. 'The inquisitors were not true Christians,' one will be told, 'and Christianity should not be blamed for the terrible things they did in its name.' But can it really be said that the inquisitors were not true Christians? For my part, I feel it is not for me, as a Buddhist, to say who is a Christian, true or otherwise, and who is not. The inquisitors, like the crusaders and the bad popes, claimed to be Christians, and I feel I have to take the claim at its face value. Similarly, it is not for me to say what Christians really believe. They say it clearly enough when they recite the Apostles' Creed, and I have to take it that they mean what they say. If I want to find out the extent to which my own beliefs, as a Buddhist, are in agreement with those held by Christians, I shall therefore have to take a look, not at some selective, sanitized version of Christianity that exists only in someone's imagination, but at the Christianity that dominated the life and thought of Europe for more than a thousand years, and which faith finds definitive expression in the certain form of words. I shall have to take a look, in other words, at the Apostles' Creed.

As I found when I recited the Apostles' Creed for the first – and last – time, the Christian begins by affirming his belief in the existence of God.

> I believe in God, the Father Almighty, Maker of heaven
> and earth:

The Nicene Creed, common to the Eastern and Western churches, not only substitutes 'one God' for 'God' but adds on 'and of all things visible and invisible' – presumably in the interest of greater clarity. I do not wish to offend or shock my Christian friends, but I have to admit that to me this article of the Christian faith is meaningless. Though I understand the meaning of the words *as words*, I am unable to connect them with any intelligible idea. I think I must never have believed in God, even as a child. In my early teen years I responded emotionally to the white-robed, compassionate figure of Jesus as evoked in the moving sermons of the minister of the Baptist church I attended, but talk of God left me completely cold. When I first encountered the Buddha's teaching I therefore was not dismayed to find that there was no place in it for an almighty Creator. For the same reason, unlike many Victorians, eminent and otherwise, and not a few Western Buddhists, I never had to go through the painful process of losing my faith in God, and with it my faith in Christianity.

Christians and other believers in God have sometimes asked me what proof I had that God does not exist. I have usually replied that it was not for me to prove to their satisfaction that God does not exist but for them to prove to mine that he does, and so far none of them have succeeded in doing this. None of the arguments I have heard or read, whether the argument from the necessity of there being an uncaused first cause, or the argument from design, or the intellectually more sophisticated argument that the idea of God necessarily involves that of his existence, have been able to convince me that such a being as God does indeed exist.

Some Christians think that one who does not believe in the existence of God, and who cannot be convinced by any of the traditional arguments, is somehow deficient in the religious sense,
but this is to identify the religious sense with the theistic sense, as
it may be called, which is merely one of its numerous forms. Not
only are there primitive societies in which the idea of an almighty
Creator is unknown; there are, also, advanced cultures that have
no word for such an idea. A Thai Buddhist once told me that
when the early Christian missionaries started translating the
Bible into the Thai language they were astonished to find it had
no word for God. They therefore coined the term 'the Buddha
who created the universe'.

The term obviously implies that there is a Buddha who has *not*
created the universe and indeed, such a Buddha – the Buddha of
the Buddhist scriptures and of Buddhist tradition – does exist.
This Buddha, who is the supreme object of Buddhist faith and
devotion, and going for Refuge to whom makes one a member of
the Buddhist community, possesses various attributes. He is
boundlessly compassionate, in that he feels love for all suffering
sentient beings, perfectly pure, in that he is free from all mental
defilements, and infinitely wise, in that he knows what leads, and
what does not lead, to the state of complete freedom from suffering, or Nirvana; but unlike the God of Christian belief he is neither omniscient nor omnipotent. Nor is that all. The state or
condition of ultimate reality, by virtue of his transcendental
knowledge of which the man Gautama became the Buddha, the
Enlightened One, boundlessly compassionate, perfectly pure,
and infinitely wise, does not stand in the relation of cause,
creator, or source to the universe or, in the words of the Nicene
Creed, all things visible and invisible.

But if the Buddha did not create the universe, then who did
create it? Someone must have created it. And anyway, why is
there no place in Buddhism for an almighty Creator? Such are the
questions one is sure to be asked should one try to explain
Buddhism to those who are new to its teachings, as I have often
found, both in India and the West. But Buddhism has a question

of its own to ask in return, one might say, a question of a more fundamental nature than these in as much as it challenges the assumptions on which they rest. It asks whether it is really necessary to believe in an almighty Creator and whether, in any case, we really need to know how the universe came into being. In what are probably the oldest Buddhist scriptures the Buddha is emphatic that his teaching has only one aim. That aim, he declares, is to point out the way that leads to the attainment of Enlightenment or Nirvana and make clear what beliefs and practices will help, and what not help, those who seek to follow that way to the end. Beliefs and speculations regarding the origin of the universe are irrelevant so far as that aim is concerned, and it is principally for this reason that belief in the existence of an almighty Creator has no place in Buddhism. Some misguided Western Buddhists would like to fill what they see as a God-shaped hole in the Buddha's teaching with a sanitized version of the traditional Christian idea of God, just as some Hindus would like to fill it with the Vedantic notion of Brahman. I have generally referred such persons, when I encountered them, to Helmuth von Glasenapp's excellent study *Buddhism – a Non-Theistic Religion*.

The Buddha also declares, in the same scriptures, that the origin of the universe or 'world' cannot be perceived. It cannot be perceived because perceiving mind and perceived object are correlative, so that however far back in time the mind travels it can never reach a point where there is no object to be perceived, that is, where there is no universe or world. Hence the Buddha also declares that within this six-foot body of ours is the origin and cessation of the world. In other words, the world 'ceases' when the subject-object duality is transcended and there is no world to be experienced by the defiled-mind consciousness, as it was later termed. Paradoxically, the beginning of the world is 'perceived' when there is no one to perceive it.

In view of these facts I have to recognize that at least so far as the first article of the Apostles' Creed is concerned there is no agreement between my own beliefs, as a Buddhist, and the beliefs held by Christians.

> And in Jesus Christ his only Son our Lord,

The Nicene Creed's version of this article of the Christian faith is much longer and more elaborate, as though to preclude all possibility of misunderstanding. It runs, 'And in one Lord Jesus Christ, the Son of God, begotten of the Father, only-begotten, God of God, Light of Light, God of very God, begotten not made, of one substance with the Father, by whom all things were made, both those in heaven and those on earth.' The principal point to emerge from this welter of words is that Jesus is not merely the 'anointed one' (*christos*) or Messiah, as in the synoptic gospels, i.e. the gospels according to Sts Matthew, Mark, and Luke; he is also God, as in the Fourth Gospel, the Gospel According to St John. Since I do not, as a Buddhist, believe in the existence of God it follows that I cannot see Jesus as God incarnate, especially as identified, in the famous prologue to the Fourth Gospel, with the *logos* or Word that was in the beginning, that was with God, and was God, by whom all things were made, and without whom nothing was made that was made (John 1:1–3). I can, perhaps, see Jesus as a Jewish religious teacher, but that is quite another matter. Christians see him as God, and since I cannot see him in this way my beliefs, as a Buddhist, are again not in agreement with those held by Christians.

> Who was conceived by the Holy Ghost, Born of the
> Virgin Mary,

With this article of faith we come to the Holy Ghost or Holy Spirit, the third member of the divine Trinity, the two other members, God the Father and God the Son being the subjects, respectively, of the first and second articles of the Apostles' Creed. So far as I have been able to make out, the Holy Ghost is a person, not an impersonal influence, in the sense in which the Father and the Son are persons, though 'orthodox' Christian theologians are careful to warn us that in this context the word 'person' is to be understood in an analogical, not a univocal, sense. Yet although the Holy Ghost is a person and not an impersonal influence, in the art of the Western Church, at least, he is not represented in the same kind of way that the Father and the Son are represented. Whereas the latter are boldly anthropomorphized, the Holy Ghost is depicted in the form of a white dove. It is as a white dove that he appears in depictions of the Trinity, balancing on outstretched wings between the Father and the crucified Son; it is as a white dove that John the Baptist sees him descending on Jesus after he has baptized the latter in the River Jordan; and it is as a white dove that he hovers over the meekly bowed head of the Virgin Mary as she receives from the angel Gabriel the news that she is to be the mother of Jesus.

Sceptics have questioned whether Jesus really was born of a virgin, on the grounds that parthenogenesis is unknown among vertebrates, being confined to such lowly life forms as plant lice and water flies. The Christian Church seems to have believed in the Virgin Birth from very early, even apostolic times, though there was also a tradition current among the Jews – attributed by the Christians to malice – that Jesus was the illegitimate son of a Roman soldier named Pathera – a view that has been adopted by some modern writers. The Church naturally regards the Virgin Birth as a miracle, though according to at least some theologians it is not so much that a miracle took place as that it had to take place. It had to take place because the pre-existing Word taking human flesh was an event unique in history, and as such it demanded a unique beginning, just as it was to have a unique consummation on earth in the Resurrection. Thus the Virgin Birth is implied by the Incarnation, and since, as a non-theistic Buddhist, I do not see Jesus as God I am unable to share the Christian belief in the Virgin Birth, even if I were to be convinced that parthenogenesis was possible in the case of the human female.

The Nicene Creed does not add anything to the above two articles of the Apostles' Creed, on the Holy Ghost and the Virgin Birth. It has in their stead a quite different article, which runs, 'Who for us men and for our salvation came down and was made flesh and lived as Man among men'. The idea of the descent of the Divine to earth in order to help and save humanity is by no means peculiar to Christianity. In some of the best-known verses of the *Bhagavadgītā*, perhaps the most popular of all Hindu scriptures, Sri Krishna tells Arjuna:

> Though I am unborn, of imperishable nature, and though I am the Lord of all beings, yet ruling over my own nature I am born by my own delusive power (*maya*). Whenever there is a decline in religion (*dharma*), O scion of Bharata, a predominance of irreligion (*adharma*), then do I manifest myself. For the protection of the good, and the destruction of the wicked, and for the firm establishment of religion, I am born age after age.[3]

Thus whereas in Christianity the Divine descends only once, in Hinduism there are many such descents or *avatāras*, to use the Sanskrit term, which in fact literally means 'descents'. There is a standard list of the ten avatāras of Vishnu from the Meena or Fish avatāra to Kalki, the avatāra who is yet to come and who will destroy the mlecchas, the foreigners, barbarians, or non-Āryans. Sri Krishna, who in the course of the eighteen chapters of the *Bhagavadgītā* gives Arjuna a complete course in Hindu religion and philosophy, is eighth in the series, coming between the hero-king Rama and the Buddha, whom Hindus recognize as an avatāra of Vishnu and Buddhists do not. It should be noted, incidentally, that the dharma of which Sri Krishna speaks is not dharma in the Buddhist sense. According to the commentary of Śaṅkara, the founder of Advaita Vedanta, the dharma of which Sri Krishna speaks is dharma as embodied in the institution of the four castes (*varna*) and four stages of life (*āśramas*), 'which are the means of attaining prosperity and salvation'.

The idea of descent or avatāra is not unknown in Buddhism. The Buddha – or rather the Buddha-to-be – also descends; but he descends not from the Absolute or Unconditioned but from a

3 *Bhagavadgītā* iv.6–8.

heavenly realm. According to Buddhist tradition, the Buddha-to-be prepared himself for the attainment of Supreme Enlightenment by practising the virtues of transcendental generosity, morality, patient endurance, energy, meditation, and wisdom for many hundreds of lifetimes. He is eventually reborn in the Tushita heaven. There he stays until it is time for him to descend. He descends in the form of a white elephant and is born as a son to Suddhodana, a Śākyan nobleman, and his wife Māyādevī, the Śākyans being a people living on the southern flank of the Himalayas, within the borders of the kingdom of Kosala. Thus unlike Sri Krishna, whose historicity is highly problematic, the Buddha is an historical figure, who lived and taught within a definite historical context. Christians believe that the founder of their religion, too, was an historical figure, a figure who, in the words of the next two articles of the Apostles' Creed,

> Suffered under Pontius Pilate,
> Was crucified, dead, and buried.

Pontius Pilate was Procurator of Judea in the reign of the Roman emperor Tiberius, so that when the Christian asserts that Jesus suffered 'under Pontius Pilate' he is affirming his belief in the historicity of the founder of his religion and, at the same time, affirming his belief in the reality of the Incarnation. For the Christian the question of whether Jesus actually did live 'as Man among men' is not one that is open to discussion. It is an article of faith, the truth of which may be supported by, but is in no way dependent on, empirical evidence. Thus it is not so much that the Christian does not doubt the historicity of Jesus as that he cannot doubt it, for to doubt it would be to undermine the entire Christian scheme of redemption, in which God descends to earth in order to save mankind.

For me the question of whether Jesus actually did live is very much one that is open to discussion. As a Buddhist, I have no emotional vested interest in its being decided either way, or in its being decided at all. Were it to be proved 'beyond reasonable doubt' that Jesus actually did live, I would not find it difficult to believe, given the fact of his existence, that he really was 'crucified, dead, and buried', crucifixion being the common mode of execution for criminals in the Roman empire at the time. What I cannot believe is that the Jewish religious teacher who was crucified was in fact no other than God, the Almighty Creator.

But what of the historicity of the Buddha? And even if the founder of the Buddhist religion actually did live, as seems to be beyond reasonable doubt, could it not be argued that for the Buddhist it is as much an article of faith that Gautama was the Buddha, the Enlightened One, as it is for the Christian that Jesus was God Incarnate? Buddhists certainly do believe that Gautama was the Buddha, the Arhant free from greed, hatred, and delusion, but their faith is of a fundamentally different kind from the faith Christians have in God, the Incarnation, the Virgin Birth, and so on. And it is a pity we have to use the same word for both kinds. The difference consists in the fact that the faith of the Buddhist is capable of verification. It is verified when, through practice of the traditional spiritual disciplines, faith is gradually transformed into transcendental knowledge. The disciple no longer needs to believe, for having attained Enlightenment as the Buddha did, he now is himself the embodiment of that which formerly was the object of his faith. The faith of the Christian is capable of no such verification. He can never become God, an idea he would regard as blasphemy. He can only believe, and trust that his belief will be suitably rewarded.

It is possible for one to have an intellectual grasp of the Buddha's teaching, up to a point, without believing the truth of that teaching. But one cannot practise it without faith – faith that Gautama was indeed the Enlightened One, the Buddha, and that his teaching, the Dharma, indeed leads to the attainment of Enlightenment or Nirvana by the disciple. 'Faith is the seed' the Buddha therefore declares in the *Sutta-nipāta*. Unfortunately, that seed seems not to have found lodgement in the hearts of some Western Buddhists. Although the Buddha made it perfectly clear that attainment of Enlightenment is inseparable from the entire cessation of greed, hatred, and delusion, such Buddhists maintain that this is not in fact the case. They believe it is possible to attain Enlightenment and yet to go on giving way to anger, for example, just as one did before, a view which leaves me wondering what kind of enlightenment they could possibly have in mind. They appear even to believe that the complete eradication of greed, hatred, and delusion is beyond human capacity, thereby implying that Gautama was not what he claimed to be, the Buddha or Enlightened One, and that it is therefore not possible for us to have faith in him as such, or in his Dharma as leading to Enlightenment. I am therefore also left wondering what kind of Buddhists they are. The Buddha would no doubt have regarded such views as wrong views, and warned those holding them that they were heading in a downward direction.

Which serves to bring us to the next article of the Apostles' Creed, which is:

He descended into hell;

The Nicene Creed has nothing to say about this, but I have seen a number of Russian icons in which the event is depicted, so I assume that the descent into hell is an article of faith within the Eastern as well as within the Western Church. In these icons a white-robed Christ breaks down the doors of hell, despite Satan's protests, and releases from limbo the souls of Adam and Eve, the patriarchs and prophets, and the just who died before his birth. I also remember reading, in my early teens, a Mystery Play known as the *Harrowing of Hell*, the existence of which suggests that in the English Middle Ages the idea of Christ's descent into hell occupied a place in the popular religious consciousness, along with the Creation and Fall of Man and the Deluge, on which there are also mystery plays. So far as I am aware, the Buddha never visited the hells (plural in Buddhism), though his disciple Maudgalyāyana is said to have visited the realm of the *pretas* or hungry ghosts. There is, however, in the Mahāyāna, the figure of the great 'mythical' Bodhisattva Kṣitigarbha, represented in Chinese and Japanese Buddhist art as a monk bearing a beringed monastic staff, who out of compassion visits the various hells in order to bring to their denizens the light of the Buddha's teaching.

Thus both Buddhists and Christians believe in the existence of a post-mortem state or place of suffering in which souls or beings experience the consequences of the evil they have done while on earth, consequences determined by the law of karma, according to Buddhism, or decreed by the Divine Justice, according to Christianity. There is another difference between Buddhist and Christian beliefs regarding the existence of such a state or place, a difference which is, if anything, of an even more fundamental character. In Buddhism, the being who is reborn in hell suffers there only for so long as the force of the karma – his own karma – which has resulted in his being there is not exhausted. Once it is exhausted, he is reborn into a different state or place, perhaps into the human world. In Christianity, the soul that is sent to hell stays there for ever. 'All hope abandon, ye who enter here' are the dreadful words inscribed above the entrance to Dante's Inferno.

The idea of eternal punishment in hell is surely one of the most horrible ideas ever to have entered into the mind of man, yet belief in its truth seems to have been an article of faith within what was to become mainstream Christianity from the beginning, and to have scriptural authority behind it. In the Gospel According to St Mark Jesus speaks repeatedly of hell and of 'the fire that never shall be quenched' (Mark 9:43–48), while at the end of the 'Little Apocalypse' in the Gospel According to St Matthew he says with regard to the Last Judgement, 'Then shall he say also unto them on the left hand, Depart from me, ye cursed, into everlasting fire, prepared for the devil and his angels.... And these shall go away into everlasting punishment; but the righteous into life eternal' (Matthew 25:41,46). Few people who have seen Michelangelo's 'Last Judgement' in the Sistine Chapel can forget the giant, almost Herculean figure of Christ the Judge and the terrible finality of the tremendous gesture of dismissal with which he sends those on his left plunging headlong into hell with expressions of horror and terror.

In the 'Little Apocalypse' it is those who have offended against charity who are sent to hell, but in his First Letter to the Corinthians St Paul greatly extends the list of offences for which one can be so condemned. 'Be not deceived:' he writes, 'neither fornicators, nor idolaters, nor adulterers, nor effeminate, nor abusers of themselves with mankind, Nor thieves, nor covetous, nor drunkards, nor revilers, nor extortioners, shall inherit the kingdom of God' (1 Corinthians 6:9–10). Not to inherit the kingdom of God means, presumably, to be sent to hell. It is clear in any case that St Paul believes in hell, for in his First Letter to the Thessalonians he speaks of the Last Judgement in much the same way that Jesus does, assuring his correspondents that God will 'Recompense tribulation to them that trouble you: And to you who are troubled rest with us, when the Lord Jesus shall be revealed from heaven with his mighty angels, In flaming fire taking vengeance on them that know not God, and that obey not the gospel of our Lord Jesus Christ: Who shall be punished with everlasting destruction from the presence of the Lord, and from the glory of his power' (2 Thessalonians, 1:6–9).

All this was understood quite literally by the early Christian writers. They believed that hell was eternal, that the suffering of the damned was without end, and that the flames with which they were punished were of material fire. It was only with the appearance of Origen, the great Alexandrian philosopher and theologian, in the third century, that some rays of light were thrown into this dismal scene. Origen, one of the most attractive figures in the history of Christianity, taught that hell was not eternal and that the souls of the wicked were not punished for ever. Indeed, he believed that their punishment was remedial; it was a purifying power, the sole purpose of which was to purify them and prepare them for eventual admittance to heaven. Origen's hell is therefore really a purgatory, like its Buddhist equivalent. He also believed in the pre-existence of the soul and in world cycles, so that it is not surprising that his Christian contemporaries should have regarded him with mixed feelings or that his subsequent influence should have been negligible. Mainstream Christianity went on its way without him, so that, to this day, most Christians believe that the punishment of the souls in hell is without end.

An idea as horrible as this naturally gave rise to some horrible emotions. In some parts of the Christian world it was considered a refinement of revenge if one could not only kill one's enemy but kill him when he was in a state of mortal sin, so that his soul would go straight to hell. Thus when the eponymous hero of *Hamlet* finds the king at prayer he decides not to kill him just then. For, he reflects,

> A villain kills my father, and for that
> I, his sole son, do this same villain send
> To heaven.
> O, this is hire and salary, not revenge.
> He took my father grossly, full of bread,
> With all his crimes broad blown, as flush as May;
> And how his audit stands who knows save heaven?
> But in our circumstance and course of thought
> 'Tis heavy with him: And am I then reveng'd,
> To take him in the purging of his soul,
> When he is fit and season'd for his passage?
> No!
> Up, sword; and know thou a more horrid hent:
> When he is drunk asleep, or in his rage,
> Or in th'incestuous pleasure of his bed,
> At gaming, swearing, or about some act
> That has no relish of salvation in't,
> Then trip him, that his heels may kick at heaven
> And that his soul may be as damn'd and black
> As hell, whereto it goes.[4]

Here we see, in the cultivated Renaissance prince, primitive desire for revenge coexisting with Christian belief in heaven and hell, the latter providing him, perhaps, with a rationalization for his inaction over his father's death.

4 *Hamlet*, Act III, Scene 3.

But Hamlet's mention of heaven brings us back to the Apostles' Creed, and to the Christian's belief that

> The third day he rose again from the dead, ascended into heaven, and sitteth on the right hand of God the Father Almighty; From thence he shall come to judge the quick and the dead.

So far as I know, it has never been shown that it is possible for a human being to come back to life after being really dead, and to come back, moreover, of their own accord. It is therefore difficult for me to believe that Jesus, having been 'crucified, dead, and buried', could have risen from the dead, whether on the third day or any other day. For me to believe that he really did rise from the dead I would have to be convinced (1) that it was possible for human beings to come back to life of their own accord and (2) that there was reliable empirical evidence that Jesus had done just that. Christians believe in the Resurrection not so much because they believe in the credibility of the rather contradictory gospel accounts of the event, as because they believe, as I as a Buddhist do not believe, that Jesus was God, and that, being God, he had power over death, as he had shown when he raised Lazarus from the dead, saying, 'Lazarus, come forth' (John 11:43). As for the Ascension, this article of faith presents difficulties even for some Christians. Given that it was the physical body of Jesus that rose from the dead, was it this same body that ascended into heaven? If it was, heaven must be located somewhere within the material universe. But if, on the other hand, he ascended in a spiritual body, then at what point was his physical body transformed into the spiritual body that ascended into heaven? For my part, I see both the Resurrection and the Ascension as belonging to mythology rather than to history, though this is not say that as myths they may not have their own spiritual significance and value, a significance perhaps better communicated by art than by the bald affirmations of an official creed.

The Apostles' Creed concludes with a series of articles not found in the Nicene Creed, except for the first of them, in which the believer affirms his faith in the Holy Ghost, the third member of the Trinity.

> I believe in the Holy Ghost; the Holy Catholic Church;
> The communion of Saints; The Forgiveness of Sins; The
> Resurrection of the body, and the life everlasting. Amen.

Since the Holy Ghost is God, as are the Father and the Son, it follows that I can no more believe in his existence than I can in theirs. Similarly, I cannot believe in the Holy Catholic Church, though this is not merely on account of the Church's moral record, bad as that record has frequently been, but on account of its claim that it was founded by Christ himself, God incarnate, when he told St Peter, the first pope, that he was the rock on which he would build his church and that he would give him the keys of the kingdom of heaven (Matthew 16:18–19). The fact that I cannot share the Christian's belief either in the Holy Ghost or the Holy Catholic Church does not, however, mean that I cannot share, to a limited extent, his belief in two other articles in the series, namely the ones relating to the forgiveness of sins and the life everlasting. But before I take a look at them I want to take a closer look at the workings of the Holy Ghost.

It was the Holy Ghost that descended upon the apostles at Pentecost, causing them 'to speak with other tongues, as the Spirit gave them utterance' (Acts 2:4), just as it causes Pentecostalist Christians to speak with tongues today. It was the Holy Ghost who, according to the Creed of Epiphanius, 'spake by the prophets', as when the prophet Isaiah, for example, prophesies that 'a Virgin shall conceive, and bear a son' (Isaiah 7:14), or when Job testifies to his faith in the resurrection of the body, saying that at the latter day 'with in my flesh shall I see God' (Job 19:26). Both 'prophecies' are based on a misunderstanding, even on a mistranslation. What Isaiah actually wrote was that 'a young woman (*almah* in the original Hebrew) would conceive, and bear a son', apparently referring to a happy event shortly expected to take place within the royal household; while Job says exactly the opposite of what his translators, from St Jerome onwards, make him say, his words actually being either 'out of my flesh' or 'without my flesh', as Froude pointed out more than a hundred and fifty years ago. Christians traditionally set great store by such prophesies and revelations, believing that the fact that they predicted events in the life of Jesus and anticipated articles of Christian faith proves that their authors were divinely inspired and that God does indeed intervene in human history.

Belief in the forgiveness of sins is not one of the articles of the Nicene Creed, though the doctrine appears to be universal in Christianity, whether Eastern or Western, Roman Catholic or Protestant. But what is sin, who is it that forgives, and in what does forgiveness consist? The short answer to these questions, so far as I have been able to make out, is that sin is transgression of the known will of God as embodied in, for example, the Ten Commandments; that it is God who forgives, as well as men; and that forgiveness consists in the remission, on repentance, of the penalty which otherwise would have been incurred. There is very little in all this with which I, as a Buddhist, can agree. To begin with, there is the idea of sin as the transgression of the known will of God, a being who for Buddhism does not exist. If there is in Buddhism a concept corresponding, roughly, to the idea of sin, it is *akusala-kamma* or 'unskilful action' of body, speech, and mind, action which has as its natural consequence unpleasant or painful experience in this life, in a future life or lives, or in both. According to Buddhism unskilful action is rooted in greed, hatred, and delusion, the threefold hub on which revolves the Wheel of Life, and these may be seen as corresponding, collectively, to the Christian idea of original sin, a state of sin innate in mankind as descendants of Adam. Christians believe that they are redeemed from sin by the sacrificial death of Jesus on the Cross, Buddhists that they can overcome greed, hatred, and delusion, and attain Enlightenment or Nirvana, by following the Noble Eightfold Path. In the Fourth Gospel John the Baptist says, as Jesus comes towards him, 'Behold the Lamb of God, which taketh away the sin of world' (John 1:29). In the *Dhammapada* the Buddha says, 'By you must the zealous effort be made. The Buddhas are only proclaimers of the Way.' (*Dhammapada* 276)

It is only with regard to the forgiveness of one man by another that there is any agreement between Christianity and Buddhism. In the Lord's Prayer, which I learned as a small child and can still repeat, Christians ask God to forgive them their trespasses 'as we forgive them that trespass against us'. For me, as a Buddhist, I forgive someone when I feel no hatred for him on account of the injury he has done me and have no desire for retaliation or revenge. The Buddha indeed goes so far as to tell his renunciant disciples, 'Bhikkhus, even if bandits were to sever you savagely limb by limb with a two-handled saw, he who gave rise to a mind of hate towards them would not be carrying out my teaching'. Nor is it enough that this should not give rise to a mind of hate. The Buddha continues:

> Herein, bhikkhus, you should train yourself thus: 'Our minds will remain unaffected, and we shall utter no evil word; we shall abide compassionate for their welfare, with a mind of loving-kindness, without inner hate.'[5]

The fact that I forgive someone does not, however, mean that by virtue of my forgiveness they will escape the karmic consequences of their unskilful action. The Buddha also says, 'Not in the sky, nor in the midst of the sea, nor yet in the clefts of mountains, nowhere in the world, in fact, is there any place to be found where, having entered, one can abide free from the consequences of one's evil deeds.' (*Dhammapada* 127.) The law of karma does not forgive.

Since Christians believe in eternal punishment in hell for the wicked it is natural that they should also believe in 'life everlasting' in heaven for the righteous. As a Buddhist I can believe in neither. According to Buddhism, sentient beings are born in heaven or hell according to the nature of their previous karma, whether predominantly skilful or predominantly unskilful, and when the force of that karma is exhausted they are reborn in other realms of conditioned existence. No life in any such realm lasts for ever.

5 *Majjhima Nikāya* i.129.

Now that I have taken my look at the Apostles' Creed it is clear to me that hardly any of my beliefs, as a Buddhist, are in agreement with the fundamental beliefs of mainstream Christianity. Only in connection with the existence of post-mortem states of happiness and suffering, and the need for men to forgive, is there agreement even to a limited extent. I was also greatly struck by the fact that in the Apostles' Creed the Christian affirms his belief in certain theological doctrines, as well as in the historicity of certain events, not in any ethical principles. It could, of course, be argued that the ethical principles derive from, and are dependent on, theological doctrines, and Christianity is not lacking in ethical teachings, such as those given in the Sermon on the Mount (Matthew 5–7), but in the Apostles' Creed, as in all the other ancient creeds, it is the theological doctrines that are highlighted.

Such highlighting is symptomatic of the Christian Church's preoccupation, during the first four or five hundred years of its existence, with giving precise theological expression to its fundamental beliefs. All the creeds, in fact, are intensely theological, and none more so than the latest of them, the Athanasian (probably late fifth century CE), the forty or more clauses of which are devoted mainly to expounding the exact nature of the relation between the three persons of the Trinity, 'neither dividing the persons nor confounding the substance', and with asserting that Jesus Christ, while indissolubly one in person, was simultaneously fully divine and fully human.

The Athanasian Creed also contains a stern warning, a warning that in the version included in the Church of England's Book of Common Prayer reads, 'Whosoever will be saved: before all things it is necessary that he hold the Catholic Faith. Which Faith except every one do keep whole and undefiled: without doubt he shall perish everlastingly.' The literal meaning of the word catholic is 'universal; relating to all men; all-inclusive', so that the 'Catholic Faith' is the universal faith, the faith held by all Christians; but this is just what the Athanasian Creed is not. Like the Apostles' Creed and the Nicene Creed, it represents the faith only of some Christians. It represents the faith of Christians belonging to the Western Church, its doctrine of the double procession of the Holy Ghost – from the Father *and* the Son – making it unacceptable to the Eastern Church. In the case of the Nicene Creed it did not represent the faith of all Christians living at the time of the First Council of Nicea (325 CE), at which the creed was formally adopted. What it represented was the faith of the party within the Christian Church that was favoured by the emperor Constantine – the party that was to become the Roman Catholic Church. That the Nicene Creed was the creed of a party, albeit a large and influential one, is shown by the fact that the Council condemned Arius and his teaching, a teaching according to which the Son was not of one substance with the Father, as the Nicene Creed maintained, but was a created being subordinate to the Father.

Thus the Nicene Creed defined not only what for its supporters was the true Christian faith but also, conversely, what for them was not the true faith. Henceforth Christians who did not keep that faith 'whole and undefiled', as the Athanasian Creed puts it, were not true Christians, not members of the Catholic Church, and would perish everlastingly. Nor was this all. The very existence of such 'heretical' Christians threatened the unity of the Holy Catholic Church, and if they could not be persuaded to submit to the authority of that church and to accept the Nicene Creed they were to be excommunicated, persecuted, and even killed, while their books were to be burnt wherever found. Among the thousands of books thus destroyed there were not only original writings by 'heretical' theologians of various persuasions but also a number of 'heretical' gospels, accounts of the life and teaching of Jesus other than the four recognized by the Church and included in the New Testament. Yet try as the Church might, it could never entirely extirpate heresy. In every generation new heresies would arise, and old ones be revived, as men insisted on thinking for themselves about the nature of the Christian faith. The list of those holding views opposed to the views of the Church was therefore a long one and included Montanists, Arians, Donatists, Priscillians, Pelagians, Nestorians,

Adoptionists, Cathars or Albigensians, Anabaptists, Lollards, Hussites, and Waldensians.

Over the years I have come to know something about all these alternative Christianities, as they should rightly be called, and especially about the Cathars or Albigensians, whose story so moved me that in 1981 I visited Carcassonne, and had circumstances permitted would also have visited their mountain fortress of Montségur, which was sacked in 1244 by the combined forces of the Church and the French crown and more than two hundred perfecti burnt. It was only the Waldensians who were no more than a name to me. As I have recently learned, their Church was founded in 1170 by Peter Waldo, a merchant of Lyon. They lived in voluntary poverty, refused to take oaths or shed blood, and later rejected certain Roman Catholic doctrines, including transubstantiation. Though often persecuted, they spread to many parts of Europe, and in the seventeenth century were still to be found inhabiting the Luserna and Angrogna Valleys on the Italian side of the Cottian Alps. In 1655 an army of 15,000 men invaded the valleys, sent by the 'Council for the Propagation of the Faith' in Turin, consisting of the chief councillors of State and Church dignitaries, the Waldensians having refused to abjure their ancestral faith and become Roman Catholics. Altogether 1,712 Waldensians were slaughtered, including women and children, thus occasioning Milton's famous sonnet 'On the late Massacher in Piemont', with which I had long been familiar without knowing just who the innocent victims were.

> Avenge O Lord thy slaughter'd Saints, whose bones
> Lie scatter'd on the Alpine mountains cold,
> Ev'n them who kept thy truth so pure of old
> When all our Fathers worship't Stocks and Stones,
> Forget not: in thy book record their groanes
> Who were thy Sheep and in their ancient Fold
> Slayn by the bloody *Piemontese* that roll'd
> Mother with Infant down the Rocks. Their moans
> The Vales reodubl'd to the Hills, and they
> To Heaven. Their martyr'd blood and ashes sow

> O're all th'*Italian* fields where still doth sway
> The triple Tyrant: that from these may grow
> A hunder'd-fold, who having learnt thy way
> Early may fly the *Babylonian* wo.

The 'triple Tyrant' is the pope, who wears a three-tiered crown, as God the Father does in some medieval altarpieces. At the time of the massacre the reigning pontiff was Alexander VII, but responsibility for the holocaust cannot be ascribed to any one person, however eminent. It must be ascribed, ultimately, to the fundamental character of the Catholic Church, with its conviction that the Christian faith can be permanently enclosed within a particular form of words, its horror of heresy, and its readiness in the past to have recourse to violence and bloodshed in support of its claims.

CHAPTER
FIVE

CHRISTIAN MYTHOLOGY

WHEN I WAS TWELVE MY PARENTS GAVE ME A COPY of Milton's *Paradise Lost* for Christmas, thus giving me what I have elsewhere described as 'the greatest poetic experience of my life'. Since then I have read the poem repeatedly, not often reading it straight through, but dipping into it here and there, revisiting favourite passages and discovering new beauties in familiar lines.

Looking back on my initial experience of the poem, I see that I read it – as I have continued to read it – in the same spirit that I would later read a play by Shakespeare or a novel by Dickens. While I was engaged in reading the work the characters represented in the one or described in the other would be very real to me, and I would respond emotionally to what they said or did, or what befell them, as though they actually existed. At the same time I would be quite aware that those characters existed only in the fertile imagination of their creator, as that imagination was bodied forth in the play or novel, or in my own imagination to the extent that it was able to participate in the imagination of Shakespeare or Dickens through the enjoyment of their work. There could be no question of my being able to experience the presence of Ariel independently of *The Tempest* or that of Mrs Gamp independently of *Martin Chuzzlewit*. Outside those works they did not exist. Like Isaac Watts' rose in winter, they had essence but not existence. Similarly, for me the principal characters in *Paradise Lost* existed only in Milton's imagination, and in my own imagination to the extent that I was able, through my enjoyment of the poem, to participate in his. For me, outside the poem they did not exist.

There is a great difference, however, between a play like *The Tempest* or a novel like *Martin Chuzzlewit* on one hand, and mythology on the other. Both the play and the poem are the work of an individual of genius, but a mythology is the product of the collective imagination of a whole people. An individual cannot create a mythology single-handed, as Blake tried to do in *The Four Zoas*, though a poet may make use of images drawn from a particular mythology, as Goethe made use of Christian images in the closing scenes of the second part of *Faust*. Every people has, or has had, a mythology of its own creation. Thus there are the mythologies of the Sumerians and the Egyptians, the Greeks and the Romans, the Indians and the Chinese, the Celts and the Teutons, the Aztecs and the Incas, and so on. Probably there is no people, however few in number, without a mythology. A people without a mythology is a people without a soul.

Religions also have their mythologies, which in some cases are simply one of its parts, along with ritual, doctrine, and a code of ethics, and in others virtually identical with it. *Paradise Lost* is Milton's poetic version of Christian mythology, just as the *Divine Comedy* is Dante's poetic version of the same mythology. Milton's version is a Protestant version, Dante's a Roman Catholic one, the principal difference between the two versions being that in *Paradise Lost* there is no place for Purgatory and no place for the glorified Madonna of the Roman Catholic collective imagination.

A mythology has been defined as 'a set of stories about gods and other supernatural beings, with whom humans may have relationships.' In *Paradise Lost* the principal supernatural beings are the Eternal Father, the Son, various angels and archangels, such as Michael, 'of celestial armies prince', Raphael, the 'affable archangel', and Uriel, 'regent of the sun', together with Satan, 'the infernal serpent', leader of the rebel angels, now become devils, among whom are Moloch, Belial, and Mammon. The humans are Adam, the first man, and Eve, the first woman, though many others are briefly mentioned in the course of Raphael's rapid survey of human history from the fallen Adam and Eve down to the Deluge, and from the Deluge down to the Crucifixion.

Milton certainly believed in the objective existence of the Eternal Father, the Son, and all the other supernatural beings of his poem, though it is unlikely that he believed they existed exactly as he had described them. For me, however, they exist only for as long as I am reading the poem. They have no existence outside it. I am therefore able to read *Paradise Lost* in the same way that I read the *Iliad* and the *Odyssey*, the only difference being that whereas it is at least 1,500 years since anyone believed in the existence of Homer's gods and goddesses, millions of people still believe in the supernatural personages of Christian mythology. Perhaps in 1,500 years' time people will be reading *Paradise Lost* as they now read the *Iliad* and the *Odyssey* and as I and other lovers of English literature already read Milton's great poem. Perhaps its mythology will prove to be the most enduring part of Christianity.

Because I read *Paradise Lost* as I read the *Iliad* and the *Odyssey*, I am free to respond to the Eternal Father and the rest of Milton's supernatural beings, as I am free to respond to Homer's gods and goddesses, without being constrained by theological considerations. The Eternal Father is not a very attractive character. No doubt Milton believed in him, even worshipped him, and no doubt he lavished on him all resources of his art; but the Judeo-Christian conception of God was a datum beyond which he could not or would not go. His angels are a very different matter. They are among Milton's most beautiful creations, especially Raphael, 'the sociable archangel', whom the Eternal Father sends to earth to converse with Adam 'as friend with friend' and warn him that Satan is plotting his and Eve's downfall. Having traversed the vast distance between heaven and earth,

> At once on th' eastern cliff of Paradise
> He lights, and to his proper shape returns,
> A Seraph winged. Six wings he wore, to shade
> His lineaments divine: the pair that clad
> Each shoulder broad came mantling o'er his breast
> With regal ornament; the middle pair
> Girt like a starry zone his waist, and round

Skirted his loins and thighs with downy gold
And colours dipped in Heaven; the third his feet
Shadowed from either heel with feathered mail,
Sky-tinctured grain. Like Maia's son he stood,
And shook his plumes, that heavenly fragrance filled
The circuit wide.

Milton's angels were probably the first with which I became acquainted. They must have made a strong impression on me, for I started drawing pictures of individual angels, notably the archangel Michael, whom I depicted hovering with outstretched wings and brandishing a sword. Angels with swords and lances also appeared in the background of a very large drawing I made of Thomas à Becket receiving the archiepiscopal ring from Pope Alexander III, which astonished my teachers not so much on account of its angels as because of my knowledge of the word 'archiepiscopal'. These angels were all Miltonic angels, as was the angel who, in the opening lines of the epic poem I was writing, appeared in my bedroom, though by this time I was also acquainted, thanks to the Tooting Public Library – with Fra Angelico's very different angels, with their high-waisted pink, blue, or green gowns, their gold aureoles, and gold or multi-coloured wings. The next angelic encounter took place in Barnstaple, at the vicarage where, as a fourteen-year-old evacuee from London, I was billeted for a while. Above my bed there hung a large monochrome reproduction of a painting depicting not one but four angels. As I discovered later, the original was the work of Sir Joshua Reynolds, and had been very popular in the Victorian period, when reproductions of it were to be seen on the walls of many a pious home. It depicted four very beautiful children's heads, all clustered together, each head being equipped with a pair of little wings.

Why I should have been so fascinated by angels I do not know. Perhaps it was because of all the supernatural beings of Christian mythology they are the ones nearest to us (apart from the devils, of course), occupying as they do a realm intermediate between the human world and the Divine. Or perhaps the bright, beautiful winged forms fascinated me because they corresponded to something deep in my own nature, something as yet hidden and undeveloped. I was therefore on the lookout for books about angels as well as for pictures of them, but the only book I came across at this period was the *Celestial Hierarchies* of Dionysius the Areopagite, which I read, in a translation by the Editors of the Shrine of Wisdom, at about the same time that I realized I was a Buddhist. Dionysius the Areopagite, whom Christian tradition identified with St Paul's Athenean convert, an identification that served to confer immense authority on his works, was in fact a Christian Neoplatonist, probably a Syrian, writing under the influence of Proclus (412–487 CE), the great pagan Neoplatonist, or one of his successors. In the *Celestial Hierarchies*, Dionysius describes the angels as being divided into three groups each with three subdivisions (Seraphim, Cherubim, and Thrones; Dominions, Virtues, and Powers; Principalities, Archangels, and Angels), each group being nearer to the Divine than the group below, the Seraphim being nearest of all, with the Angels having below them in the chain only mankind. Milton does not make use of this scheme in *Paradise Lost* but he adopts Dionysius's nomenclature, using it rather loosely, as when he refers to Raphael, who is a Seraph, as 'the affable archangel'.

That I had realized I was a Buddhist, and was reading as much Buddhist literature as I could lay my hands on, meant that it was not long before I encountered the devas, the Indian equivalents of the angels of Christian mythology. In the Buddhist scriptures, devas often visit the Buddha, usually at night. The introduction to the *Mangala Sutta*, for example, tells us that once, when the Blessed One was dwelling near Sāvatthi, at Jeta Grove, in Anāthapiṇḍika's Park, 'a certain deva of wondrous beauty lit up the Jeta Grove, and coming to the Blessed One saluted him and stood to one side.' During my long stay in India, deepening my understanding of the Buddha's teaching, I discovered that the devas were not the equivalents of the angels in all respects. Whereas the angels were created by God out of nothing, the devas were human beings born into this or that heavenly world as a result of the good deeds they had performed while on earth.

According to Buddhist tradition there are altogether twenty-two classes of devas, from those known as the Four Great Kings up to the devas who are beyond both perception and non-perception, and including the devas of limited radiance, of unlimited radiance, and of splendid radiance, who between them make up the 'celestial hierarchy' of Buddhism. Only two of these devas are commonly represented in Buddhist art, one being Indra, the other Mahabrahma, who are often seen escorting the Buddha as he descends to earth down a stairway of gold, silver, and crystal after instructing his deceased mother in the Abhidhamma in the heavenly realm into which she had been reborn.

But perhaps the true Buddhist equivalents of the angels, at least of Dionysius's angels, are the Bodhisattvas of the Mahāyāna. Dionysius says nothing about the angels having been created *ex nihilo*. In a sense they were not created at all. Though his language is obscure, it would seem that for Dionysius the different orders of angels are so many manifestations of various attributes of the Divine, each order transmitting to the one below it what he calls the Providential Stream. This downward-flowing Life has a threefold operation. It is perfective in the first group of angels, illuminating in the second, and purifying in the third. Moreover, each order of angels has an inner connection with every human soul, by virtue of which each soul is able, with their help, to purify, illumine, and perfect itself. Similarly, what I have elsewhere termed the Bodhisattva hierarchy, and described at some length, consists of five 'orders', the first being the nearest to the Dharmakāya or Absolute Bodhicitta, the fifth the farthest from it. The first order is that of the Bodhisattvas who are direct emanations of the Dharmakaya; the second, that of the Buddhas who after attaining Enlightenment retain their Bodhisattva form; the third, that of the Irreversible Bodhisattvas, who have reached the higher stages of the Bodhisattva Path and cannot resile from it; the fourth, that of the Bodhisattvas of the Path, who have reached the lower stages of that Path and can resile from it; and the fifth, that of the Novice Bodhisattvas who in principle accept the Bodhisattva Ideal but who have not reached the first stage of that Path. Through these orders there runs the golden thread of the Bodhicitta or Will to Enlightenment, absolute in the first two orders, real in the third, effective in the fourth, and preparatory in the fifth. In 1958, inspired by the beauty of the Bodhisattva Ideal, I wrote a poem entitled 'The Guardian Wall', of which the first verse was

> With sweet compassionate faces,
> Hands outstretched, humanity's friends,
> Up to the golden Zenith
> The Hierarchy ascends.

In 1962, two years before my return to England, I received from one of my Tibetan teachers, himself widely revered as a living Bodhisattva, the eighteen major and forty-six minor Bodhisattva precepts.

Once back in England, and again having access to public libraries and art galleries, it was not long before I resumed my acquaintance with the angels and other supernatural beings of Christian mythology. I soon noticed that there were as many kinds of angels as there were artists who painted them. Fra Angelico's angels were very different from Raphael's, Botticelli's from Leonardo da Vinci's, El Greco's from Delacroix's, William Blake's from Cecil Collins'. They all had wings, golden white, or multicoloured, most had haloes or aureoles, and they were generally depicted as beautiful youths or boys with long, curling hair, some of whom played on musical instruments, some sang, some fluttered aloft in the air, while others were of those concerning whom the murmuring poet was admonished that 'They also serve who only stand and wait.' But perhaps the greatest and most significant difference I saw as I turned the pages of an art book or visited, over the years, the churches and art galleries not only of my native land but also of Italy and Germany, France and Spain, was in the expressions of their faces. Some were serene, some joyful, some pensive almost to the point of melancholy. There were looks of ineffable sweetness, looks of calm, majestic dignity, and looks of tender compassion. It was as though when the artist painted the face of an angel he was painting his own soul, or at least what his soul aspired to be. In the case of those angels – and there were not a few of them – whose expressions were vacant, or coarse, or sentimental, and who therefore were not really angels at all, despite their wings and haloes, it was as though the soul of the artist was spiritually underdeveloped, however excellent his technique might be.

No angel is solitary. Except when sent on an errand to earth, they live in companies or orders, and it is as companies that I have sometimes seen them. Their natural place is in heaven, where they sing the praises of the Almighty, as in Milton's great poem, or, as in Fra Angelico's vision of paradise, where they dance upon flowering turf, among fruit-bearing trees, dancing circle-wise with graceful movements and holding each other's hands. They also assemble in large numbers on special occasions, as when the Virgin Mary is assumed bodily into heaven, or when, on another red-letter day in the celestial calendar, she is crowned Queen of Heaven, and Queen of the Angels by the Trinity, a white-robed Father and a red-robed son doing the crowning together, when the Holy Ghost in the form of a white dove hovers above their heads and a blue-mantled Virgin, her hands clasped in prayer, gazes up at the light streaming down from above, as in El Greco's painting of the event in Toledo.

But I have most often seen individual angels in contact with certain favoured persons, for Christian mythology, like all the other mythologies of the world, is 'a set of stories about gods and other supernatural beings, with whom humans may have relationships'. Raphael and Gabriel are particularly prominent in this respect. In the Book of Tobit, one of the apocryphal books of the Old Testament, Raphael the 'affable archangel', assumes the name and appearance of Azarias and accompanies Tobias, Tobit's son, from his home in Nineveh to the city of Rages, whither his strangely blinded father has sent him to collect some money. In Rages Tobias marries Sarah, and with Raphael's help overcomes the demon who has killed Sarah's seven previous husbands on their wedding night, and returns home with Raphael, Sarah, the money, and his faithful dog, who has accompanied him throughout his journey. Raphael then rewards Tobit for all his good deeds by restoring his sight, reveals his true identity, and returns to heaven.

I have seen many paintings of 'Tobias and the angel'. My favourite is the one by Verrocchio in the National Gallery, which I have seen a number of times. A curly-headed young Tobias strides along arm in arm with Raphael, who is half a head taller, the fingers of his right hand resting lightly on the angel's left wrist. He is stylishly clad in a dark-blue pleated jerkin, tightly belted at the waist, with scarlet sleeves and scarlet stockings, his dark-blue cloak billows out behind him. The artist has depicted Raphael not as Azarias but in his true angelic form, complete with multi-coloured wings and gold halo. Over a white gown he wears a plum-coloured cloak, one corner of which he holds in his left hand. Tobias looks up at him with a bright, trusting expression, while his little woolly dog keeps close to the angel's feet. Some Western Buddhists see the painting as an image of *kalyāṇa-mitratā* or 'spiritual friendship', a relationship in which the older acts as a mentor to the younger man, and which the Buddha once declared to be not the half but the whole of the spiritual life.

Tobias and Raphael are not always depicted walking arm in arm along the road to Rages, the river Tigris winding its way in the distance. In 1984 I saw at the Royal Academy's 'Genius of Venice' exhibition a very different painting of the two travellers. It was by Savoldo, and I wrote a poem on it:

> He sits at ease upon the rocks,
> The Angel with the outspread wings;
> Loosely to limbs of noblest mould
> His rose and silver vesture clings.
>
> Watchful he sits, right arm half raised
> In monitory gesture sweet,
> While travel-worn the small grey dog
> Sleeps darkling near his naked feet.

> Caught by that gesture as he kneels
> Tobias turns, as in a dream;
> Knowing his destined hour is come
> The great fish gapes from out the stream.

The 'stream' is the Tigris, and the 'great fish' the one that Tobias catches on Raphael's instructions (in Verrocchio's painting the fish is quite small, and dangles from a string held in Tobias's left hand). With the smoke of the fish's heart Tobias will exorcise the demon who had killed Sarah's previous husband, while its gall will be used to cure Tobit's blindness.

In this very popular religious short story, as it has been called, Raphael acts as the guardian angel of Tobias. Belief in the guardian angels is common to Christianity and Judaism and, within its own theological parameters, to Islam as well. All human beings have guardian angels of their own, who watch over them, protect them from harm, and encourage them to do what is good. Nations and cities also have their guardian angels. Indeed, in some esoteric and magical systems the planets, the seasons, the months, the days of the week, the hours of the day, as well as hills, mountains, and herbs, all have their guardian angels, which perhaps suggests that everything in Nature has a subtle and invisible – even a spiritual – side to its existence. In Christian mythology, the guardian angel watches over a human being from the time of his birth, a belief that Jesus himself appears to endorse when he warns the disciples, 'Take heed that ye despise not one of these little ones; for I say unto you, That in heaven their angels do always behold the face of my Father which is in heaven' (Matthew 18:10). The image of angels that behold the face of the Father puts me in mind of the passage in *Paradise Lost* in which Milton says of God as he sits 'High Thron'd above all highth' in the pure Empyrean;

> About him all the Sanctities of Heaven
> Stood thick as starrs, and from his sight received
> Beatitude past utterance.

For Milton, as no doubt for Jesus too, angels had, as we would say, an objective existence. They were not products of the human imagination. But the guardian angel, at least, can be viewed as the better, or higher, self of the individual – the self that it is possible for one to become and which, 'in heaven', one already is.

I have never actually seen an angel (though I have seen other supernatural beings), but I did once hear what I described to myself at the time as an angelic voice. Nearly forty years ago I was on the point of committing a certain act when a voice said in my ear, clearly and distinctly, 'Don't.' The voice was indescribably soft and gentle, without the least emphasis or insistence. It did not order a command. Yet it was impossible not to obey it, and I at once refrained. A few days later I learned that by refraining, and not doing what I had intended to do, I had saved myself from suffering some very unpleasant consequences. I was convinced at the time, and remain convinced, that the angelic voice I heard came from without, not from within; it was not the product of my imagination. What, then, could it have been? Was it akin to the daimon of Socrates, which on occasion told him what he was not to do, but never what he was to do? Or was it the Buddhist equivalent of the guardian angel – a deva or a Bodhisattva – watching over me and preventing me from harming myself?

The guardian angels belong to the ranks of the good angels. In fact 'good angel' sometimes means guardian angel. But there are also bad angels. There are devils. There is Satan. There is hell. According to Christian tradition the devils, including Satan, were originally angels. They are those angels who, having rebelled against God, were by him cast down into hell, there to suffer eternally. Some theologians believe that the angels who rebelled – a third part of the entire angelic host – rebelled at the very instant of their creation; others, that they rebelled subsequently, as in the version of the myth followed by Milton in *Paradise Lost*. Milton, like Blake, did not forget that Satan, the leader of the rebellion against God, was a *fallen angel*, one who in heaven had been known as Lucifer, the Light Bearer, who even in his fallen state retained some vestige of his original glory. As Milton finally says of him, as he is about to address his followers after their catastrophic defeat:

> he above the rest
> In shape and gesture proudly eminent
> Stood like a Towr; his form had yet not lost
> All her Original brightness, nor appear'd
> Less than Arch Angel ruind, and th' excess
> Of Glory obscur'd: As when the Sun new ris'n
> Looks through the Horizontal misty Air
> Shorn of his beams, or from behind the Moon
> In dim Eclips disastrous twilight sheds
> On half the Nations, and with fear of change
> Perplexes Monarchs.

One of Blake's illustrations to *Paradise Lost* depicts Lucifer in the glorious, six-winged seraphic form in which he was created and which he enjoyed until his rebellion and fall. So far as I know, only Blake has ventured to depict Satan in his unfallen state, though other illustrators of *Paradise Lost* may possibly have done so too.

That Milton did not forget that Satan was a fallen angel is interesting, even significant. It may be that he describes him in Book I of *Paradise Lost* as not appearing 'less than Arch Angel ruind' for reasons of poetic propriety. *Paradise Lost* is an epic poem, and an epic has to have a hero, as the *Iliad* has Achilles, the *Odyssey* Odysseus, and the *Aeneid* Aeneas. God could hardly be that hero, nor could Messiah, despite his victory over the rebel angels, and Adam certainly could not. That left Satan. Milton therefore endows him with courage, fortitude, endurance, and resourcefulness, all of which are heroic qualities. He may also have felt, in the depths of his poetic soul (though probably not as a theologian) that Satan, having been created good, could never become wholly evil or utterly lost. And it could have been on this account that Blake famously declared Milton to have been 'of the Devil's party without knowing it'. Be that as it may, there is little doubt that Milton's portrayal of Satan carries conviction, as does the way in which he portrays Moloch, Belial, and Mammon, his principal associates in the great rebellion, to each of which he assigns, in Book II of his poem, the speech appropriate to his particular character and temperament.

Mainstream Christianity does exactly the opposite. In keeping with its strongly held belief that Satan and his fellow devils are utterly evil, it consistently portrays them in the darkest colours. They are horrible, disgusting, and repulsive in the highest degree. In Dante's *Divine Comedy*, Dante and Virgil his guide, having visited eight previous circles of Hell, come to the fourth round of the ninth circle, where they see Satan. Of enormous size from mid-breast he stands fixed in ice, the torment here being that of freezing cold.

> Oh, what a sight!
> How passing strange it seem'd, when I did spy
> Upon his head three faces: one in front
> Of hue vermilion, the other two with this
> Midway each shoulder join'd and at the crest;
> The right 'twixt wan and yellow seem'd; the left
> To look on, such as come from whence old Nile
> Stoops to the lowlands. Under each shot forth
> Two mighty wings, enormous as became
> A bird so vast. Sails never such I saw
> Outstretched on the wide sea. No plumes had they,
> But were in texture like a bat.[6]

At every mouth his teeth chew and rend a sinner. The three sinners being thus tormented, Virgil tells Dante, are Judas, Brutus, and Cassius, for in this circle are punished the souls of those who betrayed their masters and benefactors. In Doré's black-and-white – mostly black – illustration of the dreadful scene, Satan has the horns, ears, and beard of a goat, long teeth, and a look of baffled rage. Even more horrible, to my mind, is the expression on Satan's half-animal face in the war-damaged fresco of the Last

6 Cary's translation.

Judgement in the Campo Santo in Pisa, which I have seen more than once. It is an expression not just of frustrated rage, but also of horror at his own situation, and a dull despair bordering on insanity.

In the Christian art of the Middle Ages and the Renaissance Satan is often seen seated in hell surrounded by his devils, just as God is seen enthroned in heaven surrounded by his angels. In Giotto's fresco of the Last Judgement in the Arena Chapel in Padua an enormous grey Satan, his arms half raised and hands each grasping a sinner, sits surrounded by his very much smaller devils, who are all of human size, though not human form or feature. They are covered in black, red, or grey hair, have half-simian faces, and they set upon the naked sinners like a pack of wild dogs, chasing them, biting and clawing them, throwing them down, and torturing them in various ways. But the devils are not confined to Hell, nor is Satan. It is Satan himself who, according to the Synoptic Gospels, tempted Jesus in the wilderness, challenging him first to show that he was the Son of God by changing stones to bread, then by casting himself down from the pinnacle of the Temple, whither the Tempter had transported him, and finally offering to give him all the kingdoms of the world and the glory of them if he would fall down and worship him (Matthew 4:1–11). It was Satan, too, who entered into Judas Iscariot, one of the twelve disciples, whereupon he 'communed with the chief priests and captains, how he might betray [Jesus] unto them. And they were glad, and covenanted to give him money' (Luke 22:3–5). One of Giotto's frescoes in the Arena Chapel depicts the episode. A black, semi-bestial figure stands immediately behind Judas, its black clawed hand on his shoulder, as he receives the money from a red-robed high priest.

Devils are in fact very much in evidence in the New Testament. Five or six years ago, having not read any of the Gospels for several decades, I read the Gospel According to St Mark straight through, and was struck by the extent to which devils and demoniacal possession entered into the story. In the very first chapter of this gospel, the earliest of the four recognized as authentic by the Church, we see Jesus ordering an unclean spirit to leave the man who was possessed, 'And when the unclean spirit had torn him [i.e. thrown him into convulsions], and cried with a loud voice, he came out of him' (Mark 1:26). News of what Jesus had done soon spread throughout the region, so that people brought Jesus all that were diseased, 'And he healed many that were sick of divers diseases, and cast out many devils' (Mark 1:34). Later on we find scribes from Jerusalem, the headquarters of Jewish orthodoxy, alleging that Jesus himself is possessed by Beelzebub, the prince of the devils, and casts out devils through him. Jesus reacts strongly to the allegation, declaring that he who says of him 'He hath an unclean spirit [i.e. is possessed]' sins against the Holy Ghost; he shall not be forgiven but shall be in danger of eternal damnation (Mark 3:29–30). Then there is the bizarre episode of the demoniac who lived among the tombs, howling and gashing himself with stones night and day, and whom no one had the strength to control. When Jesus commands the evil spirit to leave the man, and asked his name, 'he answered, saying, my name is Legion: for we are many. And he besought him much that he would not send them away out of the country.' Jesus therefore permits the devils to enter into a herd of pigs, whereupon the pigs – about two thousand in number – charge down the cliff and are drowned in the lake below (Mark 5:2–13).

As I read on, and got further into the story, I found Jesus causing an unclean spirit to leave the daughter of a Greek woman without his actually seeing the girl (Mark 7:26–30), commanding a deaf and dumb spirit to come out of an epileptic boy and not enter him again (Mark 9:17–26), and telling the disciples not to forbid those who cast out devils in his name, 'for there is no man which shall do a miracle in my name, that can lightly speak evil of me' (Mark 9:39).

By the time I finished reading Mark's gospel I had a mental picture of Jesus moving through a surreal landscape inhabited mainly by the sick, the diseased, and the insane, and swarming with devils of every kind. Satan and his devils were also to be met with in the two other synoptic gospels, in the Gospel According to St John, in the Acts of the Apostles, in the Epistles of St Paul, and in the Book of Revelation. The world of the New Testament is a world in which devils are everywhere, all of them on the look-out for opportunities for possessing, deceiving, and misleading human beings. St Paul therefore exhorts the Ephesians: 'Put on the whole armour of God, that ye may be able to stand against the wiles of the devil. For we wrestle not against flesh and blood, but against principalities, against powers, against the rulers of the darkness of this world, against spiritual wickedness in high places' (Ephesians 6:11–12). With such words ringing in their ears, and as Christianity spread throughout the Roman Empire, it was not difficult for Christians to see the gods and goddesses of paganism as devils who had taken on those forms in order to lure men into committing the sin of idolatry. This was in fact an article of belief with Christians for centuries. Milton makes extensive use of the belief in *Paradise Lost*, some of the loveliest passages in the poem being those in which, having had occasion to refer to a particular devil, he proceeds not only to tell us by what name the devil was known in ancient times but also to relate a myth or legend in which he features under that name. Thus he says of the devil who is the architect of Pandemonium, the infernal capital,

> and in Ausonian land
> Men called him Mulciber; and how he fell
> From Heav'n, they fabl'd, thrown by angry Jove
> Sheer o're the Chrystal Battlements: from Morn
> To Noon he fell, from Noon to dewy Eve,
> A Summers day; and with the setting Sun
> Dropt from the Zenith like a falling Star,
> On Lemnos th' Aegaean Ile.

But, Milton the poet having dwelt lovingly on the old myth, Milton the theologian does not omit to add:

> Thus they relate,
> Erring.

Even when describing the Archangel Raphael Milton cannot help concluding the description with a comparison drawn from classical mythology:

> Like Maia's son he stood
> And shook his plumes, that heavenly fragrance filled
> The circuit wide.[7]

From believing that the gods and goddesses of paganism were devils it was but a step to believing that their worshippers, if not devils themselves, at least were very much under their influence. Eventually, mainstream Christianity came to think that whoever was opposed to the Holy Catholic Church, or differed from it in doctrine, was an agent of Satan. Here St Paul had undoubtedly led the way. In his Second Letter to the Corinthians he denounced certain rival Christian teachers as 'false apostles, deceitful workers, transforming themselves into the apostles of Christ', adding caustically, 'And no marvel; for Satan himself is transformed into an angel of light. Therefore it is no great thing if his ministers also be transformed as the ministers of righteousness.' (2 Corinthians 11:13–15). Not many generations later, therefore, Irenaeus, author of the encyclopedic *Against Heresies*, was able to denounce the followers of Valentinius, the great Gnostic Christian teacher, in similar terms. Their theology was the devious result of Satan's own inspiration, he declares, and God will punish them: they will be consumed by fire from heaven (Elaine Pagels, *The Origin of Satan*, p.177). Fire seems to have been very much in the mind of orthodox Christians in those days, and it was not long before they were burning 'heretical' Christians alive, thus setting a precedent that would be followed for the next fifteen hundred years.

Besides dictating misleading theologies to heretical teachers, Satan and his devils busied themselves tempting ascetics like St Anthony, assuming for the purpose all kinds of horrible, menacing, or seductive shapes; invading the bodies of epileptics and

7 'Maia's son' is Mercury (the Greek Hermes), the messenger of the gods.

madmen; causing churches to collapse or their steeples to lean awry; and entering into compacts with sorcerers and witches. Medieval artists liked to depict devils as tiny black figures with horns, hoofs, and tails, and it is in such a form that one of them pops out of the mouth of a demoniac who is being exorcised by St Benedict, the father of Western monasticism, in one of Spinello Aretino's frescoes in the church of San Miniato in Florence, which I saw when I visited the church many years ago. But devils may also take on the appearance of human beings, as in a charming little painting by Sacchetti in which a devil's hoofs peep out from beneath his garments, thus revealing his real identity to an evidently suspicious hermit. Whether all such appearances belong simply to the feverish, frightened imagination of the Middle Ages, or whether there may not be discarnate 'evil' entities capable of harming human beings, are questions which are open to discussion. Whatever the truth of the matter may be, I had in 1970 or thereabouts an experience about which I still sometimes think.

The experience took place in the prosaic surroundings of the London Underground. I was travelling on the Northern Line, heading for home after taking a meditation class in town. Happening to look along the carriage, I saw a man standing in the doorway, his back towards me. Evidently he intended to get out at the next stop. The instant I set eyes on him I knew, intuitively, 'That's not a human being. That's a little devil.' I therefore kept an eye on him. He was of medium height, of slightly stocky build, and wore a dark suit. As soon as the train halted and the doors opened, the man turned round and very deliberately thumbed his nose at me, then skipped out onto the platform and ran away laughing. It was as if he was saying, 'I know you've spotted me, but you haven't caught me yet.' Later I wondered why I had spontaneously described him to myself as a little *devil*. As a Buddhist I do not believe in devils in the Christian sense of the word. I do not believe that there exist discarnate diabolical entities who are so irremeably evil as to be forever incapable of becoming good and who are, therefore, beyond all hope of redemption. A class of non-human beings called *māras* do, however, feature in the lives of the Buddha and his disciples, according to the Pali scriptures. They are wicked rather than evil, troublesome rather than really dangerous, and generally run away when recognized – just like my man on the Underground. Perhaps I described him as a *little* devil because he was more like a māra than a real Christian devil. I certainly did not see the tail protruding from his trouser leg.

The devils of medieval Christianity kept their horns, hoofs, and tails for quite a long time, until the painters of the Italian Renaissance, in particular, found it difficult to incorporate such grotesque figures into their sublime and beautiful art. Sometimes, however, they can be seen perched on the top of columns normally occupied by the statues of pagan deities, spectators rather than participants, in paintings in which an episode from the New Testament, or from the life of a saint, takes place against a background of imposing classical architecture. Thus devils never entirely disappear from the scene. Some devils, indeed, assume an aesthetically more pleasing outward form, and appear in certain Renaissance and Baroque paintings with magnificently proportioned human bodies, miniature horns, and an enormous reptilian tail. More often than not they are being pursued downwards by the Archangel Michael, who is ready to plunge his spear into the hindmost.

From devils to the Virgin Mary is both a short step and a long one. It is a short one in that she sometimes appears with Satan, in the form of a dragon, beneath her feet. It is a long – a very long – step from the devils to the Virgin Mary in that on account of her spotless purity – her complete freedom from sin, both actual and original – she is for Catholics the highest of all created beings.

I was attracted to the figure of the Virgin Mary even as a child. It must have been in the *Children's Encyclopedia* that I first saw a picture of her. Probably it was Murillo's 'The Immaculate Conception', for when, a few years later, I painted a picture of her, it was this famous painting that I had in mind. There was the same blue outer robe, the same long dark hair, the same hands crossed on the breast. I cannot remember if I gave her a crescent moon

beneath her feet, but in place of the twelve stars that often sur-
round her head, as in Velasquez's hardly less famous version of
the same subject, I gave her three red roses – one above her head
and one on either side. A few years later, not long before my
departure for India, I happened to hear on the radio, quite
unexpectedly, the words 'Blessed be the great Mother of God
Mary Most Holy' intoned by a priest, as I imagined, in the course
of a Roman Catholic service. They made a strange impression on
me. I had not known that for many Christians Mary was not just
the mother of Jesus but the Mother of God, and it was not until
some years after my return to England that I came to understand
the theological implications of the belief. Meanwhile, I had at
least one contact with her during my years in India. This was
when, in the summer of 1947, I took up the serious practice of
Buddhist meditation. A few days into the practice, I saw the
Virgin Mary – just as I had once painted her. This was not a true
vision but an eidetic image of my painting, released from my sub-
conscious mind by the pressure of the meditation.

Considering how prominent a place Mary occupies in Catholic
faith, worship, and private devotion, it is astonishing how infre-
quently she appears in the Gospel narrative. Her most important
appearances on the scene are at the Annunciation, when she
receives from Gabriel the angelic salutation, and is told she is to
conceive by the Holy Ghost and bear a son (Luke 1:26–38), and at
the Crucifixion, when with St John, the beloved disciple, she
stands beside the Cross (John 19:25–27). To depict the first of these
events has been the delight of Christian artists through the ages,
from Duccio and Cimabué to Rossetti and the Nazarenes. My two
favourite paintings of the scene are the one by Simone Martini in
the Uffizi and the one by Fra Angelico in the Prado. In Martini's
painting, against a gold background, and beneath three Gothic
arches, a white-robed angel, colourfully winged, holding an olive
branch and wreathed with olive leaves, kneels with a friendly,
eager expression before the blue-clad, seated Virgin, who shrinks
back in dismay at his message, seeming to avert her face. Fra
Angelico's painting is all cool blues and greys and warm pinks,
except on the extreme left of the picture where Adam and Eve are

being driven from a very green Garden of Eden by an angel. Framed by two slender columns and a round arch, Gabriel, in a pink robe and with gold wings, bows before a blue-manteled Virgin similarly framed, his hands crossed on his breast. She bows her head in complete acceptance of the Divine Will; her hands, too, are crossed on her breast, and a shaft of light from the top left-hand corner of the painting gently strikes her. Though depicting the same event, that of the Annunciation, the two artists have chosen to depict different moments in the event as described by St Luke. Simone Martini depicts Mary's initial shock and astonishment at the news that she is to be the mother of the Messiah; Fra Angelico, her eventual submission and acceptance of the role. 'Behold the handmaid of the Lord', she says to Gabriel, 'Be it unto me according to thy word' (Luke 1:38).

There is no mention of Mary's death in the New Testament, much less any mention of her being received body and soul into heaven, yet both events – the Dormition and the Assumption, as Catholics call them – have inspired countless paintings. The most impressive representation of the Dormition or Falling Asleep (i.e. death) of the Virgin Mary I have seen was not a painting but a kind of tableau. I saw it in Valencia Cathedral, some three or four years ago. In front of the high altar, on a catafalque draped in white satin, lay the white-robed figure of the Virgin, her crown on her head. Above her was suspended a canopy of white silk, while all around her were huge vases of white lilies. The place was very silent. It was as though a living person was lying there. Very likely I had chanced to visit the cathedral on the day, or perhaps in the week, of the Feast of the Dormition. But it was strange there were so few people about, though votive candles were burning at some of the side altars.

All too many paintings of the Assumption are unconvincing. In some, angels appear to be lifting the Virgin Mary up bodily into heaven; in others, she ascends with melodramatic gestures. Titian's *Assumption* in the Franciscan Frari in Venice is a glorious exception. It occupies a place above the high altar in the main chapel of the huge, grandly simple, Gothic structure, and is better seen than described. I saw it in 1983, and was amazed by the way in which the figure of the red-robed Virgin, her dark cloak swirling about her, soars out of reach of the disciples, soaring with outstretched arms and upturned face, a soft golden haze behind her, up to the eternal Father – soars from earth to heaven, from history into the realm of legend and myth.

Though she is Queen of Heaven and Queen of Angels, Mary likes to descend from time to time, with or without the Child, and show herself on earth. It seems she is particularly fond of the saints. Indeed, she has her favourites among them, as befits a great queen – favourites to whom she pays little visits and whom she graciously honours with gifts. Thus we again and again see her in paintings either giving a rosary to St Dominic, or a chasuble to St Ildefonso, or even squirting a stream of milk from her breast into the mouth of St Bernard, who was particularly devoted to her and who sings her praises in the third part of Dante's *Divine Comedy*, the 'Paradiso'. That Mary has a particular fondness for the saints, and even has her favourites among them, does not mean that she is not interested in Christians who lead less exemplary lives. Once she took the place of an absconding nun, so that her absence from the convent was not noticed by the other nuns; and once she stepped down from her altar to wipe the sweat from the brow of a poor juggler who had been juggling to please her – the only way of showing his devotion that he knew. There was even an occasion when she secretly opened the back door of hell, allowing some damned souls to escape, much to the annoyance of Satan, who complained bitterly to the Holy Trinity that the Virgin had infringed his ancient rights. In more recent times she has appeared to a number of people including children. A hundred and fifty years ago she appeared at Lourdes, in France, to Marie Bernadette Soubirous, a French peasant girl, to whom she revealed her identity with the words, 'I am the Immaculate Conception.'

She is the Immaculate Conception because, in the words of the papal pronouncement of 1854, she was 'at the first moment of her conception preserved immaculate from all stain of original sin'.

As the Immaculate Conception she appears alone, without the Child, robed in white and blue, and with the crescent moon beneath her feet, and it is in this form that Velasquez, Murillo, Zurbaran, and other artists, mostly Spanish, often depict her. In this form she floats free from her role as the Mother of God; she is no longer defined by her relationship to the Incarnate Word. She is Queen of Heaven in her own right, so to speak. Though orthodox theologians warn that Mary is not to be regarded as a fourth member of the Trinity, this is what she seems to have become in the Roman Catholic collective imagination. Indeed, she seems to have become rather more than that in some quarters. I remember seeing in a German museum a little figure of the Virgin, apparently a reliquary, with a door in the belly, a door that could be opened to reveal the Father, Son, and Holy Ghost within. Whether this is theologically correct or not I do not know, but there is little doubt that Mary came to acquire, especially in the form of the Immaculate Conception, some of the attributes of the pagan Great Mother of the lands surrounding the Mediterranean, thus becoming the object of the devotion formerly directed to Rhea and Cybele, Ishtar and Astarte, Isis and Artemis. No wonder, then, that during the Middle Ages churches dedicated to her should have risen all over Western Europe, even as they had risen to her non-Christian predecessors all over the ancient world. The Cathedral of Notre Dame at Chartres parallels the great temple of Diana at Ephesus, the citizens of which protested against St Paul's disparagement of their goddess with repeated cries of 'Great is Diana of the Ephesians!'(Acts 19:34)

The Immaculate Conception made her appearance in the New World not long after the conquest of Mexico by the Spanish. In 1531 she appeared to Juan Diego, a Roman Catholic convert, on the hill of Tepeyac, a site sacred to the Aztec mother goddess Tonantzin in Guadalupe (now part of Mexico city). The Virgin instructed him to tell the archbishop to build a church in her honour on that very site. The archbishop proved sceptical, and she had to work a miracle to convince him of the truth of Juan Diego's story. She caused flowers to appear on the hill, and ordered Juan Diego to take them to the archbishop in his cloak. But when he opened the cloak the flowers spilled out revealing the image of the Immaculate Conception on the cloth. The sceptical arch-bishop was convinced, the church – later a basilica – was built, and the cult of the dark-skinned Virgin of Guadalupe came to occupy a central place in the religious life of the Mexican people.

Brought up as I was in England, most of my contacts with the supernatural beings of Christian mythology have been mediated by the art and literature of the Christian West. Only occasionally have they been mediated by the art and literature of the Christian East. In more recent years I have seen two important collections of icons, one in England and one in Germany, and I have also seen the 'Art of Holy Russia' exhibition held in London and else-where in the late 1980s. This was a very different kind of religious art. There was no saccharine sweetness, no overt sensuous appeal (though colours were sometimes very rich), no idealiza-tion of the human form. Its Virgins were sad-eyed, its bearded Christs stern, its saints severe, its angels distant and rather forbid-ding. What was more, it had no time for naturalistic detail, and monocular perspective seemed to be unknown to it. Yet despite its limitations, if indeed limitations they are, the supernatural beings depicted in this strange Russian art were really not of this world. They existed in another dimension, outside time and space, a dimension of which the symbol was the gold or black background against which they were often portrayed.

But it was not in any collection of icons, or at any exhibition, that I made contact with the being who, of all the supernatural beings of the Russian Orthodox version of Christian mythology, fascin-ated and intrigued me most. I first came across her in the poems of Vladimir Soloviev, the Russian philosopher, theologian, and mystic, into whose writings I have dipped from time to time. This being was Sophia, the Divine Wisdom, in whose honour the great church of Hagia Sophia in Constantinople (Istanbul) was built by the emperor Justinian, and to whom many churches in Russia are dedicated. In icons she is shown seated on a throne, her feet rest-ing on a terrestrial globe. She is red in colour, with red wings, is clad in royal vestments, wears a crown, and carries a sceptre.

Some icons show her flanked by a dark-robed Virgin Mary, who holds a disc with the image of Christ, and a dark-robed John the Baptist. Thus she is not to be identified with Mary or with the second member of the Trinity. Similarly she is not to be identified with the Holy Ghost, who in other icons appears above her head in the form of a white dove. She is distinct from all three of them. Moreover, she is a person, just as the Holy Ghost, for example, is a person, not a mere personification of a virtue, like Justice or Fortitude.

Although the concept of Sophia, the Divine Wisdom, occupies with the concept of Godmanhood a central place in Soloviev's religious philosophy, it was as a person that he experienced her, and as a person that he describes her, and speaks to her, in his poetry. In his long poem 'Three Meetings' he describes his three encounters with Sophia, who for Soloviev is not only Divine Wisdom but also the World Soul and the Eternal Feminine. The first encounter took place in Moscow when he was nine, during a church service, after a girl of his own age had rejected his love; the second in London, in the Reading Room of the British Museum, where he was studying the history of mysticism; the third in Egypt, in the desert near Cairo. The last two encounters seem to have been visionary experiences, in which he saw the face of Sophia 'in heavenly radiance'.

Sophia, the Divine Wisdom, has been compared with the Prajñāpāramitā, or Perfect Wisdom, of Mahāyāna Buddhist thought and Tantric Buddhist spiritual practice. Both can be seen as beings as well as concepts, and as beings both are feminine in form. To what extent the Divine Wisdom of which Sophia is the embodiment resembles the Perfect Wisdom of which Prajñāpāramitā is the embodiment is a topic that would repay scholarly investigation, provided the approach was not merely academic. Whether or not it is ever investigated, the Sophia of the Russian Orthodox Church, especially as she appears in the life and thought of Vladimir Soloviev, remains for one Western Buddhist, at least, one of the most interesting of the supernatural beings of Christian mythology.

Chapter
six

Christian Ethics

I SUSPECT THAT HAD I BEEN ABLE TO WRITE the full-length comparative study of Buddhism and Christianity that I planned to write many years ago I would have found the chapter on the ethics of the two religions the most difficult to write. Buddhist ethics is comparatively simple, straightforward, and clear, standing in little need of interpretation. It is an ethics of intention, according to which the moral status of an act is determined by the nature of the volitional state with which it is performed, and it is for this reason that the ethics of Buddhism has been termed a psychological ethics. That it is an ethics of intention does not mean that it is a matter of those 'good intentions' with which the path to hell is said to be paved, for the kind of volitional state that renders an act moral (*kuśala*) necessarily includes an element of non-delusion (*amoha*) with regard to the true nature of things.

The ideal of Buddhism is the attainment of Enlightenment or Buddhahood. That state is attained by insight into, or realization of, the nature of ultimate reality, whether conceived as emptiness (*śūnyatā*), or as non-dual awareness (*advayacitta*). This insight, or realization, arises on the basis of an integrated, inspired, transformed, and radiant consciousness (the state of *samādhi*), and this in turn on the basis of a life purified by moral actions (*śīla*), i.e. actions expressive of volitional states of kindness, generosity, contentment, authenticity, and awareness. Reversing the order of these three levels of Buddhist experience, we have *śīla*, *samādhi*, and insight (*prajñā*, *vipaśyanā*), the three great stages of the spiritual path. All three stages have been divided and subdivided in various ways by Buddhist teachers of various schools.

Nonetheless, the broad outline of the path – its architectonic, as it were – remains quite clear. The intentional ethics of Buddhism thus does not stand alone. It forms an integral part of the Buddhist spiritual path. Indeed, it is the foundation of that path.

Christian ethics is a much more complex thing, at least in the eyes of the Buddhist observer. It is complex because it has more than one source. Although its principal source is the New Testament, in particular the ethical teachings of Jesus in the Four Gospels and of St Paul in his Epistles, it also draws upon the laws of the Old Testament, in particular the Ten Commandments, and upon the ideas and terminology of Hellenism, as well as being influenced by the theologies of St Augustine and the medieval schoolmen, most of whom were themselves influenced, directly or indirectly, by the ethical theories of Plato and Aristotle. The ethics of Protestantism, unlike those of Roman Catholicism and Orthodoxy, have been influenced by the main currents of modern Western thought from the eighteenth-century Rationalist Enlightenment to twentieth-century Existentialism.

The moral atmosphere by which I was surrounded as I grew up was that of Protestantism in its Anglican and Baptist forms. I was affected by it through my parents, through my teachers at school, through my membership of the Boys' Brigade from the age of twelve to the age of fourteen, and through my contact with certain elders of the Baptist church to which my company of the BB was affiliated. I breathed that atmosphere much as I breathed the air, without knowing of what elements it was composed, and without being aware how it was affecting me or even that it was affecting me at all. It was only later, after my realization that I was a Buddhist, that, comparing Buddhist ethical values with those of Christianity, I could begin to see the extent to which the latter had influenced me and were, perhaps, influencing me still.

Though my father taught me at an early age to repeat a short prayer each night before I slept, I cannot remember ever receiving any explicit moral instruction either from him or my mother. Instruction, if instruction there was, was entirely by example. My parents both had a strong sense of duty, and both were hard-working, though without being driven by the Protestant work ethic. They worked cheerfully, and could thoroughly enjoy whatever pleasures their modest means permitted. My mother's principal pleasures, apart from those of home, were seeing those of her nine brothers and sisters who still lived in London, going to the local cinema once a week with her best friend, and occasionally, with the same friend, eating out at a restaurant or attending a matinée in town. My father went to the cinema only when a nature film was being shown, or a film of historical interest, in which case he took me with him, and he hated eating out at restaurants and having to 'dress up' for the occasion. His principal pleasures were working in his garden (an extremely small one for the first eleven years of my life, until we moved), spending time with his friends, reading tales of travel and adventure, and taking the family to Wimbledon Common on Sundays and to the seaside for our annual holiday. My father was very much a countryman at heart, whereas my mother was city born and bred, and preferred the bright lights of the West End to a prospect of green fields and trees. I suspect she did not really enjoy our holidays at the seaside, except as they afforded her a week's respite from shopping, cooking, and cleaning. She never went in the sea, as she was too prudish to wear a bathing costume, an inhibition my father certainly did not share. Both my parents drank and smoked only in moderation, especially my mother, and I never heard from either of them any but the mildest of expletives. I was all the more shocked, therefore, when at the house of a friend of my own age, with whom I was accustomed to share the boys' papers I was still reading, I heard his rather notorious mother give vent to a four letter word I had not heard before but which I instinctively knew was a taboo word. I was shocked not so much by the word itself as by the ugly, vicious mood of which it was the expression.

At infant school I learned about Jesus, heard some of the Parables, but none of this had the effect of imparting to me a moral impulse, and when I rejoined junior school, after being confined to bed for two years or more, I found myself in the same position.

There must have been Scripture lessons, but I have no recollection of them, which suggests they made no impression on me, ethically or otherwise. This does not mean that a distinct moral consciousness had not yet arisen in me. It had arisen while I was still attending infant school, and its arising was connected with two incidents, both of which I clearly remember. The first incident took place when I was four or five, and it took place in the infant school playground. I deliberately hit a smaller boy, who ran away crying. I think I hit him because I did not like his jersey, with its alternate bands of white and orange. I instantly knew that I had *done wrong*, and this knowledge made me feel *guilty*.

But how was it that I *knew* I had done wrong, and why should that knowledge have made me feel guilty? I knew I had done wrong by virtue of the fact that the other boy was a human being like me, so that in hitting him I was to an extent disrupting the natural solidarity which exists, fundamentally, between one human being and another. The guilt I felt was the affective concomitant of my awareness that it was *I*, and no other, who was *responsible* for the wrong I had done the other boy. I had inflicted a wound on the body of our common humanity, and my feeling of guilt was the *pain* of that wound. No doubt I did not understand all this at the time, but the fact that I could know I had done wrong, that I could know that it was I who was responsible for what I had done, and that I could feel guilt on its account, certainly constituted, so far as I can remember, the first arising of a distinct moral consciousness in me.

I have heard it said, even by some who should have known better, that guilt is an entirely negative emotion and that one should neither feel guilt oneself nor make others feel it. This is to confuse rational guilt with irrational guilt. One experiences rational guilt when one offends against what Buddhist ethics terms natural morality (*pakati-sīla*), and irrational guilt when one fails to observe what it terms conventional morality (*paññati-sīla*). Natural morality is based on the fundamental difference that exists between those actions that are expressions of volitional states of greed, hatred, and delusion, such as killing and stealing, and those that are expressions of the opposite volitional states, such as deeds of kindness and generosity. Conventional morality is not so based. As the term suggests, it is simply a matter of social custom and observance, and is in itself morally neutral. Offences against natural morality are not only accompanied by the feeling of rational guilt; sooner or later they are followed, under the law of karma, by suffering. The most serious offence against natural morality that one can commit is the deliberate killing of another human being, an offence which brings upon the offender the most serious consequences, both social and karmic. This does not mean that the deliberate killing of animals, especially for pleasure, is not also an offence against natural morality, for it disrupts our sense of kinship, as human beings, with other forms of life, especially the higher forms. It is for this reason that abstention from killing (*pāṇātipātā veramaṇī*) is the first of both the five and the ten moral precepts of Buddhism. One who habitually breaks this precept, and who moreover experiences no feeling of guilt on that account, has sunk below the truly human level, or at least has regressed to the pre-moral condition of infancy and early childhood.

The second incident with which the arising in me of a distinct moral consciousness was connected, took place when I was six. It took place at the South London Hospital for Children, to which I had been admitted for the then routine tonsillectomy. I stayed there for two or three days, and during that time I was kept in bed, as were the other children in the ward. It once so happened that I urgently needed a bedpan, and as the nurse passed by my bed I called out to her to bring me one. But she ignored my call. In the course of the next few minutes she passed by several times, and each time I called out to her for the bedpan, but she continued to ignore my appeals, even though I called more and more loudly and insistently. Eventually, as was inevitable, I fouled the bed, whereupon the same nurse at once came over to me and scolded me vigorously for what had happened, as though it was my fault. I keenly felt the injustice of the scolding. When I hit the boy in the playground I knew I had done wrong, and I felt guilty. Now, when the nurse scolded me, I knew *she* was doing what was wrong, and I felt indignant. She had committed an offence against natural morality, for in scolding me for what had happened as though it was my fault, when it was hers for repeatedly ignoring me when I called out for the bedpan, she was acting a lie. She was refusing to accept responsibility for her action, or rather for her inaction, and 'inaction in a deed of mercy becomes an action in a deadly sin'. I did not think all this at the time, but the incident burned into my young being the consciousness that injustice is morally wrong.

My membership of the Boys' Brigade and my contact with the church to which our company was affiliated, afforded me no such incidents as the two I have described. The pastor's moving sermons served merely to inflame my religious emotions. Specifically moral instruction came only at the BB's Sunday morning Bible class and after the Friday evening drill. The instructor was our brisk, cheery little captain, who also led the prayers and the hymn-singing. The principal sins, I gathered, were smoking, drinking, and swearing. The three went together, so that if you fell victim to one sin you would almost certainly fall victim, sooner or later, to the two others. There were also exhortations to lead 'a clean life', though just what this meant was not spelled out. Sex was in fact never mentioned, either at the BB itself, at school, or within the family circle, and it was only when I was transferred to a 'better' school, at the age of thirteen or fourteen, that I heard the subject discussed – smuttily and surreptitiously – by some of the older boys. It must have been at about this time that I received the only sex education I ever had. One Sunday afternoon my father handed me his copy of *Health and Strength* magazine, and pointing to one of the articles said 'I think you should read this.' The article was about masturbation. I read it with interest, but I did not need its advice as much as my father may have thought, for I was leading as 'clean' a life as the BB could have desired. My father never asked if I had read the article, nor did I tell him I had done so. He probably thought that in drawing my attention to the article he had done his parental duty so far as that department of my education was concerned.

It must have been at about this time, too, that I became aware that I was physically and emotionally attracted to members of my own sex. Indeed, though I read the article on masturbation with genuine interest, I looked with much greater interest at the photos of well built young men, naked except for a posing pouch, that were a leading feature of the magazine. Some of them reminded me of sculptures of the Greek gods – Apollo, Hermes, and the rest – pictures of which I had seen in the *Children's Encyclopedia*. That I was attracted to older boys, and to young men, in this way, did not make me feel guilty; nor did I feel guilt when the attraction started to assume a definitely sexual character, as it did a year or two later. It was a feeling that had arisen in me quite naturally; it was part of me, and I did not question its rightness. At the same time I instinctively knew, even at that early age, that it was something of which society disapproved and that I should not talk about it to anyone.

Since I could not talk about my feeling to anyone it was several years before I discovered that there were others who were attracted to members of their own sex and that there was a name for this attraction. Enlightenment eventually came when I was about seventeen, and it came from Edward Carpenter's *The Third Sex* and from the chapter on homosexuality in Havelock Ellis's *The Psychology of Sex*, a work that has been described as 'sympathetic and scientific'. In the meantime, a lot had been happening in my life. I had left school and started work, I had realized I was not a Christian, and in the moral writings of the Roman Stoic philosopher Seneca I had breathed a cleaner, fresher moral atmosphere than that of Christianity. Above all, I had realized on reading the *Diamond Sūtra* and the *Sūtra of Wei Lang* that I was a Buddhist, and that in the depths of my being I had always been one. I also became increasingly aware, during the period of these developments, of the way in which society regarded sexual feelings such as mine. It did not merely disapprove of them. It regarded them with the utmost abhorrence, and in some countries to act upon them was a criminal offence. In 1895, only thirty years before I was born, the poet and playwright Oscar Wilde, then at the height of his career, was sentenced to two years imprisonment with hard labour for breaking the law prohibiting sexual relations between men, and that law was still on the statute book.

How had such a state of affairs come about? Why did society regard with such hostility, and punish so harshly, an inclination which, if my own experience was anything to go by, arose quite naturally, and which, as I now understood from my reading of *The Psychology of Sex*, was found in all periods of history, and in all walks of life, and not least among some of the most gifted writers, artists, and musicians. It was Havelock Ellis who provided me with a clue. Only with the coming of Christianity had homosexuality fallen into disrepute, it having been idealized by the ancient Greeks in association with intellectual, aesthetic, and ethical qualities. After the time of the Byzantine emperor Justinian (483–565 CE) it was regarded as 'a vulgar vice, or rather as a crime, deserving of the most severe secular and ecclesiastical penalties, even burning at the stake'.[8]

What had led the Christian Church to devalue, even to demonize, homosexual relations in this way? The answer was to be found, I discovered, in the Bible. Both the Book of Leviticus in the Old Testament and St Paul's Epistle to the Romans in the New, contain a passage dealing with the subject. Leviticus is short and to the point. God tells the Israelites, through Moses, 'Thou shalt not lie with mankind, as with womankind: it is abomination' (Leviticus 18:22). St Paul is more prolix, and seems almost to foam at the mouth as he delivers his diatribe against the pagans and denounces homosexuality as one of the degrading passions to which God, in his anger, has abandoned them for worshipping not him, the immortal God, but images made with their own hands, thus giving up divine truth for a lie. The key verses are, 'For this cause God gave them up unto vile affections: for even their women did change the natural use into that which is against nature: And likewise also the men, leaving the natural use of the woman, burned in their lust one toward another; men

8 *The Psychology of Sex*, p.189.

with men working that which is unseemly, and receiving in themselves that recompense of their error which was meet' (Romans 1:26–27). Probably few passages in the Bible have been responsible for as much human misery as these from Leviticus and the Epistle to the Romans.

But although I had been provided with a clue to the mystery of society's hostility to homosexuality, twenty years were to pass before I was in a position to follow that clue through the labyrinth of Christian ethics. During this time I did at least read one book that had some bearing on the subject. This was André Gide's *Corydon*, a cautious but courageous defence of homosexuality in Socratic dialogue form, which I came across in a Calcutta bookshop. I also discovered that homosexuality was not unknown in the gompas of Tibet or the viharas of South-East Asia. Though the Vinaya or Code of Monastic Discipline prohibits monks (and nuns) from engaging in sexual activities of any kind, I gathered from conversations with some of my brother monks that pederasty, at least, was generally regarded as a peccadillo rather than as a serious offence. There was also an unheralded visit from the American Beat poet Allen Ginsberg, who did not hide the fact that he had a male lover and that he was interested in exploring the possibility of practising Tantric sex 'with a boy'.

By the time I returned to England the moral climate had changed a little, at least in some quarters and in some respects. Sex was now being talked about more openly, books previously banned for their 'obscenity', like Radclyffe Hall's lesbian novel *The Well of Loneliness*, had been republished, and the newly elected Labour government was about to repeal the law under which Oscar Wilde had been convicted and replace it with one permitting homosexual acts between consenting adults in private. The Roman Catholic Church, together with the Anglican Church and other Protestant bodies, strongly opposed this more liberal attitude to homosexuality, though within each communion a few brave souls refused to toe the official line, maintaining that it was possible to be actively homosexual *and* a practising Christian. Over the years, however, even the Roman Catholic Church shifted its position slightly. It was not a sin to be a homosexual, in the sense of having homosexual feelings, but it was a sin to act in accordance with those feelings. God thus was credited with endowing some human beings with certain very powerful desires and then, for his own mysterious reasons, forbidding them to fulfil those desires on pain of damnation. The absurdity of such a position had already been the subject of an untitled, bitterly satirical poem by A.E. Housman, written around the time of the trial of Oscar Wilde but published only after the author's death in 1936.

> Oh who is that young sinner with the handcuffs on his wrists?
> And what has he been after that they groan and shake their fists?
> And wherefore is he wearing such a conscience-stricken air?
> Oh they're taking him to prison for the colour of his hair.
>
> 'Tis a shame to human nature, such a head of hair as his;
> In the good old time 'twas hanging for the colour that it is;
> Though hanging isn't bad enough and flaying would be fair
> For the nameless and abominable colour of his hair.
>
> Oh a deal of pains he's taken and a pretty price he's paid
> To hide his poll or dye it of a mentionable shade;
> But they've pulled the beggar's hat off for the world to see
>   and stare,
> And they're taking him to justice for the colour of his hair.
>
> Now 'tis oakum for his fingers and the treadmill for his feet,
> And the quarry-gang on Portland in the cold and in the heat,
> And between his spells of labour in the time he has to spare
> He can curse the God that made him for the colour of his hair.

Obviously, it is not easy for Christians to be more sympathetic to homosexuality, for the Bible evinces no such sympathy for it whatever. Leviticus categorically forbids sexual relations between men and the Epistle to the Romans represents homosexuality as the object of God's anger and classes it with all manner of wickedness, including murder. Since for Christians the Bible is divinely inspired, it follows that it is possible for them to accept homosexuality, whether in others or in themselves, only if they understand that inspiration to be of a general nature, not as extending to every sentence of every author contributing to its formation. Judging by their attitude to homosexuality, practically all the churches believe every sentence of the Bible to be divinely inspired, not culturally conditioned, and applicable to all human beings at all periods of history. The non-Christian is therefore entitled to ask the leaders of those churches about their attitude to witches, witches having been persecuted by the Church between the fifteenth and seventeenth centuries, hundreds of thousands of them having been put to death during those years. After all, the Book of Exodus's 'Thou shalt not suffer a witch to live' (Exodus 22:18) is no less categorical than the Book of Leviticus's 'Thou shalt not lie with mankind as with womankind'. Witchcraft is no longer a criminal offence in Europe, though self-styled witches still exist among us, but so far as I am aware neither the Roman Catholic Church nor any of the Protestant churches advocate the revival of the old laws against witchcraft or believe that in an ideal Christian society witches would again be put to death. Exodus 22:18 has been allowed to become a dead letter, along with many other of the Old Testament's prohibitions and injunctions. Why cannot Leviticus 18:22 be allowed to be become a dead letter, too?

The Jesus of the Four Gospels does not say anything about homosexuality, but he has quite a lot to say about how people should behave towards one another. In the course of his Sermon on the Mount (actually a later compilation of the Master's sayings) Jesus tells the disciples that their virtue should go beyond that of the Scribes and Pharisees. Not only should they not kill, they should not even get angry; not only should they not commit adultery, they should not even look at a woman lustfully; and so on. Moreover, they are to love their enemies, pray for those who persecute them, forgive others their failings, and are not to judge anyone. Above all, 'Whatsoever ye would that men should do to you, do ye even so to them: for this is the law and the prophets' (Matthew 7:12). Here Jesus emphasizes the spirit rather than the letter of morality, and the eponymous author of the Gospel reports that the people were deeply impressed by his teaching, accustomed as no doubt they were to the more legalistic moral teaching of the religious authorities. Jesus in fact is appealing to the natural sense of solidarity that exists between one human being and another, any breach of which is the real immorality. This sense of human solidarity is basis of what Buddhism terms natural morality, which in turn constitutes the ultimate basis of social morality and of law.

Christians therefore have a choice with regard to their attitude to homosexuals. They can treat them either in accordance with the letter of the Old Testament or in accordance with the spirit of the New. They can treat them with hostility, as breakers of what they believe to be a divinely revealed commandment binding on all men for all time, or they can treat them with sympathy and respect as fellow human beings. They can denounce them, and class them with criminals, as St Paul does (despite his singing the praises of love in 1 Corinthians 13), or they can behave towards homosexuals in the way in which Jesus, in the Sermon on the Mount, tells the disciples they are to behave towards their fellow men. For Jesus the Golden Rule, in its positive form, was 'the law and the prophets', and the Golden Rule by its very nature excludes no one – not even homosexuals. Unfortunately, Christians on the whole have chosen to treat homosexuals with hostility, the Church having decided early in its history, on the basis of Leviticus 18:22 and Romans 1:26–27, that sexual relations between men were a grave sin and to be punished accordingly.

Even in the Middle Ages, however, there were men who, while not questioning the Church's teaching on the sinfulness of homosexuality, were nonetheless able to feel affection and respect for individual homosexuals. Dante was such a man. In the *Divine Comedy* he represents himself and his guide, the poet Virgil, as meeting in the seventh Circle of Hell a troop of spirits. They are running along beside a river of blood, on a margin of burning sand, and are tormented by a shower of fiery rain. They are being punished for 'violence against Nature'. One of the spirits is the

Florentine scholar Brunetto Latini, Dante's old preceptor. He and Dante recognize each other and a touching conversation ensues. Dante expresses his deep gratitude to Latini, who predicts a glorious future for him if he follows his star but warns him to have no truck with the ungrateful and malignant Florentines. The other members of his troop, Latini tells Dante, were all clerics and scholars of great fame who on earth were guilty of the same crime as himself. There were so many of them that there was not time for him to relate all their histories, but he would mention three of them individually; Priscian (the Roman grammarian), Francesco, son of Accorso (an eminent lawyer), and the notorious bishop whom the Pope was obliged to transfer to another see. Continuing on their way, Dante and his guide see another troop of spirits running along beneath the fiery rain. Three of them run on ahead and circle round Dante, naked, and bleeding from the fiery rain. They were citizens of Florence distinguished in war and council, and Virgil tells Dante they deserve to be treated with courtesy. Two of them were noblemen, the third a rich man of humble birth who abandoned his savage-tempered wife for what one of Dante's Victorian translators calls 'wicked ways'. Dante tells the three that he feels not contempt but sorrow at their plight and that he has always honoured them for their patriotism. One of the spirits then inquires if courage and courtesy still abide within their native city; but Dante is unable to give them a positive reply, and the three resume their running along the burning sand.

Dante's attitude to Brunetto Latini, his old preceptor, and the rest of those who were being punished for 'violence against Nature', stands in luminous contrast to the attitude of the vast majority of Christians to homosexuals, both before and after his time. So different is his attitude that I cannot but wonder if Dante was privately of the opinion that homosexuality was not so great a sin as the Church thought, or perhaps not a sin at all. This seems all the more likely in view of his attitude to those who were being punished for usury, another form of 'violence against Nature', whom he sees at the limit of the seventh Circle. They are seated on the burning sand, vainly trying to ward off with their hands the fiery rain that falls upon them. Dante does not recognize any of them. One of them speaks to him, but he does not reply. The very least one can conclude is that Dante probably had more sympathy for homosexuals than for moneylenders. The Roman Catholic Church, of course, has long since ceased to regard usury as a sin, but homosexuality is as much a sin as ever. The same may be said of the Anglican and other major Protestant churches. They, too, have quietly dropped usury from the catalogue of sins, while continuing to regard homosexuality as one of the worst sins a human being can commit. On this subject Rome, Canterbury, Geneva, and Wittenberg all speak with one voice.

That they should do so is not astonishing, given that the attitude to homosexuality of all of them is predicated on Leviticus 18:22 and Romans 1:26–27. What is really astonishing is that Christianity should have been able, during the period of its ascendency in Europe, to implant its abhorrence of homosexuality so deeply in the Western psyche that it continued to be felt not only by Christians but even by some of those who had abandoned Christianity. It was surely one of the most successful exercises in mass indoctrination that the world has ever seen. Just how successful it was is illustrated by what happened to Oscar Wilde after his release from prison. Since it was impossible for him to live in England he went to stay in France. There, as Hesketh Pearson relates, he was treated as a moral leper to the end of his days.

> At a word from some American or Englishman, barmen would refuse to serve him drinks, restaurant proprietors would ask him to leave, hotel managers would turn him out, barbers would decline to shave him, respectable fathers would clutch their children to their sides as he passed by. Many men who had known all about his sexual oddity in the days of his success, and had been proud of his acquaintance then, now disowned him and either cut or avoided him. The English and Americans were his chief traducers and tormentors, but every self-important French writer kept out of his way, vicious little paragraphs about him appeared at regular intervals in the

French press, and only the younger and more rebellious spirits were to be seen in his company.[9]

Oscar Wilde died in 1900. Since then, and especially since the 1960s, 'the love that dare not speak its name' has increasingly found a voice; more and more people are prepared to tolerate, even if not to accept, homosexuality, and homosexuals are better able to lead free and open lives. At the same time, the picture is a mixed one. The churches, led by the Roman Catholic Church, remain implacably hostile to homosexual behaviour, which they continue to regard as a grave sin, the President of an African state has publicly denounced homosexuals as 'worse than animals', and in some parts of the world, including England, it is still possible for homosexuals to be attacked and killed on account of their sexuality. It is no accident that in the twentieth century the word 'homophobia' should have entered the language and found a place in English dictionaries, where it is defined as 'intense hatred or fear of homosexuals or homosexuality'. That hatred or fear is in part due, in the Anglo-Saxon world at least, to one-sided ideas, on the part of the heterosexual majority, of what it means to be a man; but it is also due, to a great extent, to the continued influence of the 'theological homophobia' of Christianity.

'The priest lays his curse on the fairest joys,' wrote William Blake. Friendship is one of the fairest and truest joys of life, and the Roman Catholic Church, in particular, has laid its curse on it by its stern warning against the moral dangers of what it calls 'particular friendships', that is to say, friendships between men (and between women) that are more intimate, more emotionally intense, and even more passionate, than is customary in our culture between members of the same sex. Though the warning was addressed primarily to those living in single-sex, celibate religious communities it also had a much wider application. Particular friendships were morally dangerous not only for monks and nuns but also for lay persons, especially the young and impressionable. They were dangerous not merely because they could

9 *The Life of Oscar Wilde*, pp.358–9.

lead, in religious communities, to exclusivity and factionalism; they were dangerous because sexual feelings might be aroused in the parties to the friendship and this might lead to their having (homo)sexual relations. This linkage of particular friendships with the 'danger' of homosexuality has had unfortunate consequences. It has made many men in the West, especially those brought up as Roman Catholics or under the influence of Catholicism, fearful of entering into any friendship with another man that goes deeper than casual acquaintanceship or superficial camaraderie. The result is that they are emotionally impoverished.

Some years ago I came across Aelred of Rievaulx's *Spiritual Friendship* and was so pleased with the little work that I recommended it to a number of Buddhist friends. Aelred was a twelfth-century English monk who spent the latter part of his life as abbot of the Cistercian monastery of Rievaulx in Yorkshire, the extensive ruins of which I once visited on a misty, melancholy autumn afternoon. One of the reasons I was pleased with *Spiritual Friendship* was that Aelred, unlike other abbots of his own and later times, did not allow himself or his monks to be prevented from enjoying emotional, even physically demonstrative, friendships by the bogey of homosexuality. He rates friendship very highly; he is an enthusiastic advocate of its value and importance. It is part of the moral life, and in his eyes those who seek to live without it are more beasts than men. It is also part of the spiritual life, and Aelred goes so far as to assert that 'God is friendship'. This striking assertion cannot but remind me, as a Buddhist, of the Buddha's emphatic declaration that spiritual friendship (*kalyāṇa mitratā*) was not half the holy life (*brahmacarya*), as Ānanda had supposed; it was the whole of it.

Today, after centuries of neglect, Aelred of Rievaulx's *Spiritual Friendship* is again being studied, and Catholics interested in the social implications of the Christian life are taking seriously his assertion that 'God is friendship'. Similarly, certain Western Buddhists have begun to take seriously the Buddha's declaration that spiritual friendship is the whole of the holy life, an insight which for more than two millennia had lain hidden in the depths of the Pali Buddhist scriptures, apparently unnoticed by the official custodians of those scriptures. Such Western Buddhists see the Buddhist spiritual community (*sangha*) as a network of spiritual friendships, the strength of that community being dependent on the strength of the multitudinous friendships of which the network is composed.

Just as Christians have a choice with regard to their attitude to homosexuals, so do they have a choice with regard to their attitude to non-Christians. They can behave towards them in accordance with the letter of the Old Testament, where God commands the Israelites to destroy the Amalekites (1 Samuel 15:3) and other unclean and idolatrous people (e.g. Numbers 31) or in accordance with the spirit of the New Testament as represented by the Sermon on the Mount and the Golden Rule. History shows that they have harkened more often to the commands of Jehovah than to the counsels of Jesus and that, given the power and the opportunity, they could treat non-Christians no better than they treated heretics and homosexuals. In every generation there were, of course, Christians who took the Sermon on the Mount and the example of Jesus seriously, some of them being persecuted for so doing, as the Spiritual Franciscans were by the Roman Catholic Church and the early Quakers by the Church of England.

Much of the violence of which Christians have been guilty, whether towards Muslims, Jews, South American Indians, or Vietnamese Buddhists, can no doubt be ascribed to the ignoble passions that they share with the rest of unregenerate humanity. Hence it would be not right for me, as a Buddhist, to criticize Christians for being subject to passions to which Buddhists are also subject and to which they, too, despite the Buddha's teaching, may sometimes give hurtful and destructive expression. But there is in the historical violence of Christians towards non-Christians, as well as towards heretics and homosexuals, an element that is not to be found in the violence of backsliding Buddhists, however reprehensible. It is an element that is not peculiar to Christianity but which characterizes other divinely revealed monotheistic religions. I do not find it easy to define this element, the horrifying nature of which is illustrated by a Spanish short story I once read, a story of which the following is a bald summary.

In the days of Philip II there lived in Spain a nobleman of ancient lineage who had two beautiful unmarried daughters. He was a widower, and resided with them in his ancestral mansion on the outskirts of the town. Since he possessed properties in different parts of the country, he was often away from home for weeks at a time, so that the two young women were left very much to their own devices. Visitors were of course forbidden, and since both daughters were of a serious turn of mind they spent much of their time discussing religious matters. One day the father returned home unexpectedly and on going to his daughters' room caught them studying the New Testament. When he demanded to know what this meant, for the New Testament was virtually a banned book in Catholic Spain, they confessed that as a result of reading the Gospels they had become Lutherans. Now the nobleman was a devout, even fanatical, son of the Church, and he had no words to express his horror, astonishment, and grief that they should have disgraced him in this terrible way. As was his duty, he at once reported his daughters to the Holy Office of the Inquisition. They were arrested, imprisoned, and tried for heresy, and since they steadfastly refused to renounce their new faith they were sentenced to be burnt at the stake as heretics. On the eve of the execution the father went to the Inquisitors and asked, as a particular favour, to be allowed to provide the firewood with which his heretical daughters would be burnt and to pile it up round them with his own hands. This pious request was readily granted. Two days later, after the young women had met their terrible end, the mansion in which they had lived caught fire and was burned to the ground. Their father perished in the flames, and it was rumoured that he had set fire to the building with his own hand.

I do not know whether the story is based on an historical incident or whether it is the product of the author's imagination. In any case, it was powerfully written and made a strong and lasting impression on my mind. It perfectly illustrates the nature of the horrifying element within Christian violence with which I am concerned. Morality is born from a sense of the natural solidarity of human beings with one another and, ultimately, with all forms of life. That sense is strongest in relation to those with whom we are connected by ties of blood, which is why partricide and matricide have ever been considered such dreadful crimes, even when committed unknowingly, as when Oedipus killed Laius without being aware of his real identity. In actively bringing about (with the Inquisition) the horrible death of his two daughters the nobleman in the story disrupts the natural solidarity that exists between parent and child. He thus is guilty of committing an act of the blackest immorality, and he commits it on account of his religion and with the full approval of its highest authorities. It is his religion that makes him immoral, as it has made immoral the countless Christians who, through the centuries, have persecuted and killed fellow human beings who thought, believed, or behaved differently from themselves. Why was this? What is there in Christianity that has caused Christians to behave in this heartless and inhuman fashion?

Eventually I realized that the answer to these questions lay a long way back in the history of Christianity and in the history of its predecessor, Judaism. During the two centuries following the death of Jesus there was not one Christianity but many. In the countries surrounding the Mediterranean there were scores, even hundreds, of little groups or 'churches' of believers, all having their own leaders, their own doctrines, and their own scriptures, and all competing with one another as well as with the various pagan cults. Irenaeus, the influential second-century Bishop of Lyon, in effect divided Christians into two great categories, the orthodox and the heterodox, the latter and their heretical writings being the subject of his encyclopedic *Against the Heresies*. Orthodox Christians were those who belonged to his own church, the church of which the Bishop of Rome (later to become 'the Pope') was the head and St Peter, the Prince of the Apostles, the founder. Irenaeus moreover championed the Gospel According to St John, adding it to the three Synoptic Gospels to make the 'four formed gospel', the only complete and reliable record of the life and ministry of Jesus. It is this gospel that portrays Jesus as God Incarnate, not simply as the Messiah, and represents him as saying, 'I am the way, the truth, and the life: no man cometh unto the Father, but by me,' (John 14:6) – words which have enabled Christians to insist that only through faith in Jesus Christ can anyone be saved.

By the beginning of the third century, thanks to Ireaneus, the 'orthodox' church headed by the Bishop of Rome was a well organized, centralized international body. It had a corpus of 'reliable' scriptures, a 'high' conception of the nature of Jesus, and an unswerving conviction that it alone was in possession of the fullness of Christian truth. When the emperor Constantine became a Christian it was this orthodox Catholic church that he patronized to the exclusion of all others, endowing it and its head with property, money, and civil power, thereby enabling it to persecute heretics and destroy their heretical books. There thus came into existence the Holy Catholic Church, doctrinaire, authoritarian, intolerant, and not averse to the use of violence in pursuit of its aims. In the twelfth century, after a long period of estrangement between Latins and Greeks, the Catholic Christian Church split into two great halves: the Roman Catholic Church and the Eastern Orthodox Church, a schism that was conformed by the sacking and looting of Constantinople in 1202 by the Frankish Crusaders during the Fourth Crusade. In the middle of the sixteenth century the Western Church itself split in two, one half consisting of the rump Roman Catholic Church, the other of the Lutheran, Calvinist, and Anglican churches, together with their respective offshoots. All these churches have inherited, to a greater or a lesser extent, the mindset of their remote ancestor the Constantinian Holy Catholic Church of the fourth century. It is this mindset which is responsible for that element within Christian violence which my Spanish short story illustrates. It is on account of this mindset that Christians have only too often been prepared to disrupt, in the supposed interests of their faith, the natural solidarity which exists between one human being and another, disrupting it even in those cases where it normally is strongest.

The historical violence of Christianity towards non-Christians is also due, in part, to the example of ancient Judaism. The Old Testament notoriously sanctions violence against the worshippers of other gods, and the books of the Old Testament form part of the Christian Bible. There were, however, some early Christians who believed that there was so great a discrepancy between the religious and moral teaching of the Old Testament and that of the New that they could not have issued from the same divine source. One such Christian was Marcion, the founder of Marcionism, who lived and taught in Rome in the middle of the second century and whose teachings spread to many parts of the Roman empire. According to Marcion there were two Gods, the just God of the Law and the Prophets, and of the Old Testament generally, and the benevolent God, the heavenly Father of whom Jesus had spoken. Jesus was not of human birth. He was a purely spiritual being who, descending from heaven into the world created by the just God, had suddenly appeared in Galilee (apparently as a full-grown man) in the fifteenth year of the reign of Tiberius; and he had only appeared to suffer on the Cross. Marcion regarded the Third Gospel, which he did not attribute to St Luke, as containing a reliable account of the life and ministry of Jesus, at least in part; the three other gospels he rejected out of hand for what he saw as their Judaizing tendency. In the rest of the New Testament he accepted only the Pauline Epistles.

Had other Christians cut themselves loose from the Old Testament, as Marcion and his followers did, or had Constantine patronized the Marcionites instead of the Catholics (an unlikely event in view of the kind of church for which he was looking) the history of Christianity, and with it the history of Europe, may well have been different. As it was, the Old Testament was accepted along with the New, and its sanctioning of violence in the interests of religion helped reinforce Christianity's intolerance of religious difference. This has led me, as a Buddhist, to reflect that the history of Buddhism, and with it the history of Asia, would have been very different had the Vedic literature been bound up in a single volume, so to speak, with the Dialogues of the Buddha, so that Buddhists had a choice between performing animal sacrifices, as enjoined by the Vedas, and developing goodwill (*mettā*) towards all living beings, as taught by the Buddha. Fortunately, this never happened, and rarely in the history of Buddhism has theology been allowed to subvert ethics or dogma to disrupt the natural solidarity between one human being and another.

Chapter
seven

Saints and Mystics

BIOGRAPHIES HAVE ALWAYS BEEN one of my favourite forms of literature. It was therefore to be expected that I should have read, in the course of a long life, not only the lives of poets, painters, and philosophers, but also those of Christian saints, mystics, visionaries, and prophets. I did not read the biographies of these Christian worthies for the sake of spiritual uplift and illumination, although this did sometimes come, just as it sometimes came when I read the lives of great poets, painters, and philosophers. I read their biographies because they were remarkable men and women whose lives were of intense human interest.

In my teens I encountered, thanks to their biographers, a saint, a mystic, and a prophet. The saint was St Francis of Assisi, the mystic was Mme Guyon, and the prophet was Savonarola. I have related elsewhere how affected I was by *The Little Flowers* and *The Life of St Francis*, and how when I saw a beggar standing before me I gave him all my money, just as St Francis might have done – except that St Francis probably would not have possessed any money. As so many have done, I delighted in his preaching to the birds, whom he called his little sisters, and his conversion of the fierce wolf of Gubbio. But Francis was no sentimental romantic. Poverty and humility were his two ideals, and he practised both to the utmost extent. He spoke of himself as wedded to Lady Poverty, and the closeness of that union can be seen from his worn, patched tunic, of the coarsest sackcloth, still preserved as a holy relic in an Italian church. At the same time he was no sour ascetic. Until the end, when the order he had founded started to depart from his teaching, his life was one of joy.

The nature of that joy is well illustrated by an episode in *The Little Flowers*. It was a winter's day, and Francis was going from Perugia with Friar Leo to St Mary of the Angels suffering sorely from the bitter cold. As they went, he called out to Friar Leo, who was walking before him, that even if the friars minor in every land were to give good example of holiness and edification, nevertheless he should write and note down diligently that perfect joy was not to be found therein. In the same way he called out to Friar Leo that perfect joy was not to be found in the friar minor's miracles of healing, nor in his knowing all the sciences and all the Scriptures, nor in his speaking with the tongues of angels, nor in his preaching so well that he converted all the infidels to the faith of Christ, each time telling him to write down and note this diligently. When they had gone on for two good miles in this fashion Friar Leo, in great wonder, prayed Francis in God's name to tell him where perfect joy *was* to be found. Francis answered him thus:

> When we are come to St Mary of the Angels, wet through with rain, frozen with cold, and foul with mire and tormented with hunger; and when we knock at the door, the doorkeeper cometh in rage and saith, 'Who are ye?' and we say, 'We are two of your friars,' and he answers, 'Ye tell not true; ye are rather two knaves that go deceiving the world and stealing the alms of the poor; begone!' and he openeth not to us, and maketh us stay outside hungry and cold all night in the rain and snow; then if we endure patiently such cruelty, such abuse, and such insolent dismissal without complaint or murmuring, and believe humbly and charitably that that doorkeeper truly knows us, and that God maketh him to rail against us; O Friar Leo, write – there is perfect joy.

In other words, true joy did not depend on external conditions; it was even heightened when they were adverse. Reading this episode from *The Little Flowers* again many years later, I was at once reminded of Tibet's great yogi Milarepa, who also was wedded to Lady Poverty and who, wearing only a thin cotton robe and sometimes not even that, sang songs of joy as he dwelt in the snowy mountains of his native land.

Mme Jeanne Marie Bouvier de la Motte Guyon lived in the France of Louis XIV, and as an advocate of Quietism played a prominent if controversial part in the spiritual life of her country. The dictionary defines Quietism as a form of religious mysticism requiring withdrawal of the spirit from all human effort and complete passivity to God's will, but for its opponents it is the exaggeration and perversion of the mystical doctrine of interior quiet. I do not remember much of Upham's biography of Mme Guyon, which I have not seen since my impressionable teens, but I do remember at least one thing clearly. This was Mme Guyon's doctrine of pure or disinterested love, according to which one should love God purely, without hope for heaven or fear of hell – which was also the doctrine of certain Sufi mystics. As I subsequently learned from other sources, Mme Guyon suffered for her views. Despite the championship of Fénelon, the saintly Archbishop of Cambrai, she spent many years in prison, and eventually Quietist teaching received papal condemnation. Like other forms of mysticism, Quietism was perceived as dangerous by the religious authorities, for it made a spiritual life independent of the institutional church and its sacraments.

Girolamo Savonarola was a Dominican friar, preacher, and prophet who fell foul of the religious authorities in another way. Though the contemporary of Mantegna and Piero della Francesca, Botticelli and Leonardo da Vinci, he was no 'Renaissance man' but a throwback to the Middle Ages. Shocked by the corruption he saw in Florence, where he was prior of the monastery of San Marco, a corruption he believed was due to the city's wealth and to the discovery of the pagan classics, he delivered a series of passionate sermons in which he so terrified the people with predictions of the judgement to come if they did not mend their ways that they drove out their cultivated Medici ruling family and established a Christian republic with Savonarola himself as spiritual dictator. During the carnival season of 1497 a great 'bonfire of vanities' was held, in which personal ornaments, lewd pictures, and cards and gambling tables were consigned to the flames. Botticelli, who had been deeply affected by the friar's preaching, is said to have contributed some of his own works to the holocaust. But soon a reaction set in. People grew tired of having to be virtuous. Moreover, Savonarola had made political enemies, both at home and abroad. These enemies joined forces with the Pope, the infamous Alexander VI, whom Savonarola had attacked in his sermons. In the end the populace turned against him. Savonarola was arrested, tortured, and condemned (he can hardly be said to have been tried). One year after the 'bonfire of vanities' he was publicly hanged, with his two close companions, and his body burned.

My second encounter with a saint (an uncanonized one) took place a few years later, when I was in Singapore, and it took place through the medium of the little book of his sayings and letters that was put together after his death. The saint was Brother Lawrence of the Resurrection, a French Carmelite friar who was an older contemporary of Mme Guyon, and author of the book *The Practice of the Presence of God*. Brother Lawrence was a simple man of humble birth who had been a soldier, a manservant, and a hermit before entering the Carmelite monastery in Paris, where he was employed as cook. He was not a visionary, and perhaps not even a mystic, if to be a mystic is to experience ecstasies like those of St Teresa. His spiritual practice was to remain constantly aware of the presence of God, whatever he was doing. Though I did not make the comparison at the time, Brother Lawrence's practice of the presence of God was perhaps not dissimilar to the Buddhist practice of Buddhānussati, the constant recollection of the Buddha, with or without the repetition of his attributes or of a mantra. I did, however, write an article comparing certain aspects of Brother Lawrence's teaching with the yogas of the *Bhagavadgītā*, and the article was published, in two instalments, in a Hindu religious magazine. I must have been quite touched by his sincerity and directness.

But touched though I was by Brother Lawrence's little book it had no practical consequences for my own spiritual life as a

Buddhist. Such was not the case with the book I was given by a
Roman Catholic priest four or five years later. The book was *Seeds
of Contemplation* by the Irish-American Trappist monk Thomas
Merton. At the time I was in India. I had recently become a
Buddhist monk, and with my teacher, the Venerable Jagdish
Kashyap, I was on pilgrimage to the Buddhist holy places of
Bihar. One of them was Rajgir. There, besides visiting the site of
the Bamboo Grove, where the Buddha had often stayed, we
called at the Roman Catholic mission and had a friendly talk with
the priest. When we left he presented me with two books. One of
them was *Seeds of Contemplation*. The rest of the story is best told
in the words of my first volume of memoirs.

> For some time past I had been greatly preoccupied with
> the question of ego, not only with the theoretical question
> of what it was, or was not, but with the more practical one
> of how to get round it, or get rid of it, or get beyond it.
> Meditation did not seem enough. Something more drastic
> and more down-to-earth was needed, something that
> could be practised every hour of the day, something that
> would provide a constant check to the unruly motions of
> the egoistic *will*. In *Seeds of Contemplation* I found what I
> wanted, or at least a clear enough indication of it. The
> disciple should surrender his will absolutely to the will of
> his spiritual superior. In small matters as in great he
> should have no will of his own, not even any personal
> wishes or preferences. This was the secret. This was the
> way to subjugate the ego, if not to destroy it completely.
> Though the idea was certainly not unfamiliar to me, it had
> never struck me so forcibly before, and I resolved to apply
> it forthwith to my relations with Kashyap-ji. In future his
> wishes would be my law. I would have no wishes of my
> own. Whenever he asked me if I would like to do
> something, as in the goodness of his heart he often did, I
> would reply that I had no preference in that matter, and
> that we would do just as he wished. For the remainder of
> the time that we were together I faithfully adhered to this

resolution. As a result, I had no troubles, and experienced a great peace of mind.[10]

The result was that when, our pilgrimage over, Kashyap-ji took me up to Kalimpong, in the foothills of the eastern Himalayas, and instructed me to stay there and work for the good of Buddhism, I did just that. For the next fourteen years, with Kalimpong as my headquarters, I worked for Buddhism – writing, teaching, and lecturing – in Kalimpong and the surrounding area as well as in other parts of India. Only in 1964, with the blessing of Kashyap-ji and my other teachers, did I return to England, where I seemed to be more needed.

I had not been long in England when I was introduced by Walter Nigg's *Warriors of God* to eleven more saints, all of them founders of religious orders, and all canonized. It was a thoughtful, well-written book, and although the author, a Swiss Protestant clergyman, treated the founders sympathetically, and tried to understand them, he could also be critical. They were very different from one another, and though all were officially saints some were not very attractive characters. St Pachomius, the fourth-century founder of the first Christian monastery, spoke contemptuously of Origen, the great Alexandrian theologian and philosopher, dismissing his writings as 'foolish chatter' and declaring that anyone who read his works and accepted his ideas would be consigned to the depths of hell. According to Pachomius's biographer, Pachomius could tell by a stranger's smell whether he was infected with Origen's 'heretical' ideas, which makes him seem more like an African witch doctor than a Christian monk. St Bernard of Clairvaux, the founder of the Cistercian order, who dominated the religious and political life of Western Europe for much of the twelfth century, had an even keener nose for heresy than St Pachomius. Heresy was everywhere, he complained bitterly towards the end of his life. No sooner was it stamped out in one place than it sprang up in another. He seems not to have understood that orthodoxy and heterodoxy were the obverse

10 Sangharakshita, *The Rainbow Road*, p.449.

and reverse of the same coin, and that if there was orthodoxy, and if men had minds and could think, there would inevitably be heresy. Though Nigg has much to say about St Bernard's mysticism and his intense devotion to the person of Christ, as exemplified by his eloquent sermons on the Song of Songs, he says little about his involvement in the Second Crusade. At the joint entreaty of the Pope and the king of France he travelled through France and Germany whipping up popular support for the enterprise with his oratory. Like his contemporaries, St Bernard believed that fighting the infidel was an activity highly pleasing to God. In the event, the Second Crusade was a disaster. The crusaders achieved nothing, and nine-tenths of them lost their lives.

For me, the most impressive of Nigg's 'warriors' was St Bruno of Cologne, and the Carthusian order the most remarkable of the orders they had founded. A bitter experience of the simony that was endemic in the eleventh-century Church convinced him of the vanity of the world, and he decided to become a monk. He seems also to have had a profound experience of the inevitability of death and the Last Judgement and the certainty, if one had led only a nominally Christian life, of eternal damnation. The Benedictine monastery of Molesne proving not strict enough for him, he settled with six companions in the wilds of the Dauphiné mountains. There they built the first Carthusian monastery. Unlike the monks of other orders, they did not live conventually. Each monk had his own separate cell, where he worked, prayed, and studied, and they met together only on Sunday. They rarely spoke. These verses from Ernest Dowson's poem 'Carthusians' well captures the spirit of Carthusian monastic life:

> Within their austere walls no voices penetrate;
>   A sacred silence only, as of death, obtains;
> Nothing finds entry here of loud or passionate;
>   This quiet is the exceeding profit of their pains.
>
> From many lands they came, in divers fiery ways;
>   Each knew at last the vanity of earthly joys;
> And one was crowned with thorns, and one was crowned

with bays,
And each was tired at last of the world's foolish noise.

It was not theirs with Dominic to preach God's holy wrath,
    They were too stern to bear sweet Francis' gentle sway;
Theirs was a higher calling and a steeper path,
    To dwell alone with Christ, to meditate and pray.

A cloistered company, they are companionless,
    None knoweth here the secret of his brother's heart:
They are but come together for more loneliness,
    Whose bond is solitude and silence all their part.

The Carthusian order was remarkable for its never having been reformed. It had never been reformed because it had never become corrupted. In the case of other religious orders a short initial period of rapid growth was usually followed by a much longer period of slow decline, after which it had to be revived or reformed. The Carthusians started modestly and continued steadily, and it was not until two hundred years after St Bruno's death that the order he had founded was really under way. After that, even the Great Schism could not halt it. According to Walter Nigg, the secret of Carthusian stability lay in the order's stern adherence to its ancient discipline. Connected with this was a concern for the quality rather than the quantity of its membership.

In England the Carthusians lasted until the dissolution of the monasteries under Henry VIII. Four monks of the London Charterhouse, including the prior, were executed in 1553 for treason on account of their refusal to repudiate the supremacy of the pope and recognize the king as head of the Church in England. They died nobly, but I, for one, wish they could have died for a nobler cause than that of papal supremacy. The Roman Catholic Church naturally regards them as martyrs. In 1989 I was in Spain, and happening to visit the grand Cartuja on the outskirts of Granada I saw, hanging in the monastery's refectory, several large paintings depicting the arrest, trial, and execution of the unfortunate monks. As I wrote at the time 'the paintings were well executed, and it was in any case interesting to see an episode from the history of Protestant England through Spanish Catholic eyes.'

Over the years I became acquainted with many more saints or 'warriors of God', not all of them the founders of religious orders. I came to know them not through the biographies of disciples and latter-day admirers, or through their own writings, but more often through the paintings I saw in churches and art galleries. I did not always meet them under the best conditions. St John the Baptist was being beheaded, as were St Maurice and his ten thousand companions; St Lawrence was being roasted on a gridiron; St Agatha was having her breasts cut off (sometimes I saw her holding them on a little dish); St Sebastian, tied naked to a tree, was being shot at with arrows; and St Erasmus was having his intestines drawn out with the help of a windlass. All this I found quite distasteful, especially when there was a lot of blood around. Christians seemed to be rather fond of blood. Of course, St John the Baptist and the rest had all been executed under the pagan Roman emperors, when executions were cruel and bloody affairs, so that if these martyrdoms were to be depicted at all there would have to be at least a little blood. What was more, Jesus himself had been crucified, so that if the Crucifixion, too, had to be depicted, it would have to be depicted similarly, with blood trickling from the hands and feet of the Saviour and from the wound in his side.

However, as I moved from room to room of the art galleries, and from period to period of European art, I noticed that as religious art became more realistic it also tended to be more sanguinary. In early Christian art there was no blood at all to be seen. Jesus hangs on the Cross without a single drop of blood falling from his hands or feet or from the wound in his side. Sometimes he seems not to hang from the Cross at all but rather to be laid flat on the wood, without there being any tension. Sometimes he looks straight ahead. Even in the Middle Ages, when the emaciated body of Jesus twists in agony, and his head slumps to one side, the artists of the time were not preoccupied with the gory concomitants of the Crucifixion. That preoccupation came later, reaching its apogee in some of the life-size polychrome figures of Spanish religious art. I once saw in a church in southern Spain a particularly gruesome example of the genre. Jesus has just been flogged, prior to being crucified; he is naked except for a loincloth, and his body is streaming with blood. In the interest of greater verisimilitude his loincloth is made of real cloth and his hair and beard of real hair. Crudely realistic representations of the sufferings of Jesus such as this are meant to evoke a strong emotional response on the part of the spectator, whether one of horror, or pity, or indignation, or devotion. They are also meant to make him feel guilty, for it is on account of *his* sins, together with those of the rest of mankind, that Jesus suffers.

St Jerome was not a martyr, for he was born when Catholic or 'orthodox' Christianity had just become the official religion of the Roman empire; neither was he the founder of a religious order, though one was founded in his name many centuries after his death. We often met, especially in the course of my various Italian journeys of the 1980s, when I spent as much time as I could visiting the churches and art galleries of Florence and Siena, of Venice, Rome, and Naples. Sometimes he appeared wearing – anachronistically – the broad-brimmed red hat and red robes of a cardinal, either alone or in the company of other saints. At other times he could be seen on his knees in the desert, performing penance for his sins, or seated in his peaceful study, or secluded cell, translating the scriptures. He performed his penance beneath blue skies, amidst magnificent mountain scenery, and in the shadow of fantastic rock formations. Besides the huge volumes from which he was translating, his study contained little more than a human skull and an hourglass, one reminding him of the inevitability of death, the other that time was passing and that not a moment should be wasted. Sometimes his cardinal's hat hangs on the wall. Whether outside or inside, he is attended by his faithful lion.

I particularly liked seeing St Jerome when he was translating. There were times when he worked in almost total darkness, the page over which his bald head was bent illumined by a single candle. There were times, also, when sunlight came streaming in through the window, lighting up every detail of the place. The more I saw of St Jerome in his study, translating, the more I felt drawn to him. I was drawn to him not just as an interesting historical personality who, after a varied career as teacher, traveller, hermit, pilgrim, and secretary to the reigning pope, had left Rome out of disgust at the corruption of the Roman clergy and made his way to the Holy Land, there to spend the rest of his life in literary activity. Rather was I drawn to him on account of what he represented, or embodied. With his long white beard, and venerable appearance, for me he was the embodiment of the Wise Old Man, one of Jung's Archetypes of the Collective Unconscious. That he was engaged in the work of translating, especially that of rendering the Word of God, as contained in the Hebrew of the Old Testament and the Greek of the New, into Latin, the *lingua franca* of the Roman world, meant that something hidden in the depths was being brought to the surface and the light of day. A sonnet I wrote on St Jerome in 1967, a year after my first Italian journey, concludes with the following lines:

> In a world of sin
> The Empire changes hands, the Churches fight
> Factious as dogs. By day the old man, stung,
> Magnificently answers Augustine,
> Then, dredging from the deep, night after night
> Translates THE WORD into the vulgar tongue.

Because St Jerome was 'dredging from the deep' he was the Alchemist, another embodiment of the Wise Old Man, and his study was the Alchemist's laboratory, where lead was transmuted into gold.

No doubt I was drawn to St Jerome partly because of my personal situation at the time. As I explain in a paper written in the course of my 1984 Italian journey,

I was living in the desert. I had left the 'Rome' of collective, official, even establishment, Buddhism, and was seeking to return to the origins of Buddhism in the actual life and experience of the Buddha and his immediate disciples. Not only that. I was trying to teach Buddhism in the West, which meant I was trying to communicate the spirit of the Dharma in terms of Western rather than in terms of Eastern culture. I was thus a translator, with all that that implies in the way of seeking to fathom the uttermost depths of what one is trying to translate so that one may translate it faithfully, i.e. bring its meaning to the surface, or from darkness into light. Thus I was drawn to the image of St Jerome, and was able to see that image as an embodiment of the archetype of the Wise Old Man as 'Translator' and Alchemist, because I had a personal affinity with that image, or because there was something in me that corresponded to that image.

Although St Jerome is regarded as a saint, in certain respects he was not a very saintlike person. A Christian scholar says of him, 'He was passionate and sensuous, yet he was the champion of the most rigid asceticism. Full of petty vanity and learned rivalry, he was self-assertive and unjust to his opponents; and though destitute of the creative theologian's gift, he liked to pose as a pillar of orthodoxy.' Nonetheless, St Jerome's historical importance cannot be denied, and the same authority therefore continues, 'By his translation of the Bible he exercised an immense influence upon the succeeding centuries, and in that work he produced what must be numbered among the supreme achievements of the Christian mind in any age.' Despite his being the champion of rigid asceticism, St Jerome seems to have been more scholar and littérateur than saint.

There could be no doubting the saintliness of St Catherine of Siena, who impressed me as much as St Jerome, though not as the embodiment of an archetype but as a remarkable human being. She was born in Siena, the city of the *palia* or 'banner', in 1347. On account of its romantic hilltop situation, and the fact that within its walls it remained essentially a medieval town, it was my favourite Italian city, and I visited it a number of times. I loved the Tuscan Gothic cathedral with its colourful, ornate façade, its bands of black and white marble on walls and pillars, its unique marble mosaic floor, and its many art treasures including Duccio's *Maestà*. I loved the shell-shaped main piazza with its fountain by Jacopo della Quercia, the lofty bell-tower of the flanking city hall, and the gentle, almond-eyed saints and virgins who thronged the churches and the city art gallery. I also loved the grass-grown city walls, the cavernous shops (open-fronted like those in India), and the steep, cobbled streets, in one of which I found, on my first visit to Siena, the house in which St Catherine had been born to a prosperous dyer and his wife as the last but one of their twenty-five children. Every room in the house had been turned into a chapel or oratory, with coffered ceilings and frescoed walls, and on what once had been the family's kitchen garden there stood a baroque church.

As a small child, Catherine was of a lively, affectionate disposition, but when she was seven or eight she had her first vision, and a change took place. She became silent and withdrawn, and devoted herself to prayer and penance. This displeased her parents, who sought by various means, both gentle and harsh, to induce her to give up her austerities. They desisted only when her father, entering her room one day when she was kneeling in prayer, saw a pure white dove on her head – an incident depicted in one of the frescoes, along with others relating to her early life. When Catherine was sixteen she was received as a Penitent of the Third Order of St Dominic, and henceforth wore the black and white habit of the Order. She continued to live at home, occupying the tiny room that had become her cell, and giving herself up to a life of extreme austerity, not to say self-mortification.

On leaving the House and Sanctuary of St Catherine, as the complex was called, I made my way up the steep acclivity that led to the tall, brick-built Dominican church that occupied the top of the hill, dominating the narrow streets below. The first thing I saw on entering the building was the preserved head of the saint, behind glass, high up on the wall, it having been separated from her body shortly after her death and sent to Siena from Rome, where she had died and where her body was still preserved. In the gloom of the church it was just possible to make out the features. More appealing than this grisly relic was the portrait by Andrea Vanni, a friend and admirer of the saint, that hung in a little chapel to which the saint had often come to pray, and where she had been received as a Penitent. She wore the white robe and black mantle of the Order, the white symbolizing innocence and the black humility. In her left hand she held a lily, while her right hand was presented to a female votary kneeling at her feet, who seemed about to kiss her fingers. The expression with which the saint looked down at the votary was calm and thoughtful. There were other paintings in the chapel, all of them depicting scenes from Catherine's life, and all by Bazzi, also known as Sodoma. The most beautiful of them depicted the saint being supported by two nuns as she swoons in ecstasy, overcome by some mystical experience. It seemed incredible that this slight, delicate young woman, with what the Victorian author of a sketch taken from Vanni's portrait described as a 'spare, worn, but elegant face, with small, regular features', should not only have engaged in the most fearsome austerities, in the midst of which she experienced both spiritual raptures and terrible diabolical temptations, but should also have played, for eight years of her short life, a central, even pivotal, part in the religious and political life of Italy.

In the middle of the fourteenth century much of Italy was in turmoil. There were wars between rival city states, as well as bitter, bloody internecine strife in the case of some of them, including Siena. Roving bands of mercenaries plundered and looted, and there was the arrival from the East of the Black Death, with its appalling economic and social consequences. The turmoil extended to the Church. Morals were lax, not least among the higher clergy, and simony and nepotism were rife. Worst of all, in 1308 the reigning pope had moved from Rome to Avignon in France, and at the time of Catherine's birth the papacy had been based there for forty years, with the result that Rome, no longer the capital of Christendom, had become a city of ruins haunted by thieves and murderers. It was into this turmoil that Catherine threw herself when, at the age of twenty-five, she began what she called her 'mission to the world'. By this time a small band of disciples had formed around her and she had gained a widespread reputation for sanctity. Her mission began with an impassioned letter to a leading cardinal, the pope's representative in Italy, in which she sang the praises of charity, in the sense of selfless love of others, as the true foundation of social harmony and political stability. That Italy should be at peace was her greatest earthly desire. When Gregory XI called for a Crusade against the Muslims she therefore gave the idea her enthusiastic support, apparently seeing it as a means of ridding Italy of the marauding mercenary bands, and wrote to princes and prelates all over Europe urging them to take up the Cross. Neither princes nor prelates wanted to take part in the Crusade, however, and preparations for the enterprise never got off the ground. Catherine realized that peace would come to Italy only if the pope returned to Rome, and in the course of a visit to Avignon she was able to persuade him, despite strong opposition from the French cardinals, to take this momentous step.

In 1377, amid general rejoicing, Gregory entered the eternal city and took up residence in the Vatican, thus bringing to an end the papacy's 'Babylonian Captivity' in Avignon. A year later he died, to be succeeded by Urban VI. The new pope had been elected under duress, the Romans having threatened to kill the cardinals if they did not give them a Roman or at least an Italian pope, and it was not long before a group of cardinals met at nearby Fondi and elected another pope, Clement VII. Christendom now had two popes, and later would have three, each anathematizing and excommunicating the two others and their adherents. Catherine regarded Urban as the true pope, and did her utmost to persuade the adherents of Clement to accept him as such. Amid these stirring events she reconciled deadly enemies, comforted the sick and bereaved, and consoled the dying, as she had done ever since leaving her cell for the world. In this connection there occurred, towards the end of the saint's life, an incident which strikingly illustrates her character. Niccolà di Tondo, a young

Perugian noble, had been unjustly sentenced to death by the government of Siena for uttering some rash words against the state. Mad with despair, he refused to make his confession or to listen to a word about the salvation of his soul. But when Catherine visited him in his cell and spoke to him he calmed down and accepted his fate. She was with him to the last, as she had promised him she would be, and received his severed head into her hands as it fell from the block. Then to her ecstatic gaze the heavens seemed to open and she saw the Saviour, in likeness like the sun, receive the victim's blood into his own open wounds.

In 1378, having finished dictating her *Dialogue*, a mystical treatise, the saint left Siena for Rome, where she was received with great honour by Urban, and where she helped reorganize the Church. Two years later, still living in Rome, she died, worn out by her austerities and her labours in the cause of peace. She was thirty-three. In 1461 she was canonized by Pius II, a fellow Sienese. The event is commemorated in one of the brilliant frescoes with which Pinturicchio, with the assistance of the young Raphael, decorated the walls of the Piccolomini Library in Siena Cathedral. Wearing the papal tiara, his right hand raised, Pius sits enthroned aloft, beneath a canopy, flanked by his red-robed cardinals. The body of Catherine, habited in the Penitent's white and black, lies stretched out on a catafalque at his feet, her head slightly raised. Below, in the foreground, monks, nuns, and lay people stand holding lighted tapers.

Today St Catherine of Siena's body lies, behind glass, beneath the high altar of Santa Maria sopra Minerva, one of the finest of the old basilica churches of Rome. I have twice seen her there, and it seemed to me that there emanated from her, in death as in life, that same 'fragrant purity' of which one of her disciples spoke.

St Bridget of Sweden had died in Rome seven years before St Catherine did. She lived there for twenty-three years. Unlike St Catherine she had been married and had children before becoming a nun, and unlike the Italian saint she had founded a religious order, that of the Sisters of the Most Holy Saviour or Brigittines. In other respects these two saints were very much alike. St Bridget, too, had practised severe austerities, had seen visions and received revelations. Many of the revelations related to the corruption of the times, especially the corruption of the Church, and called for reform. Some called for the return of the pope from Avignon to Rome, a cause for which St Bridget worked as enthusiastically as St Catherine did after her, if with less success. Her visionary experiences included a vision of the crucified Saviour which influenced her whole life and outlook. She seems to have been more visionary than mystic and more prophetess than visionary, receiving from God messages in which princes and prelates were threatened with dire consequences if they did not mend their ways. As a visionary she cannot be compared with a fellow countryman of hers who lived five hundred years later, in whose name there was founded, after his death, not a religious order but a new church, the Church of the New Jerusalem.

Swedenborg was born in Stockholm in 1688 and died in London in 1772. He had a distinguished career as scientist, philosopher, and civil servant in the course of which he had published a number of works of a philosophical or scientific nature, some of them quite substantial. But in 1744, when he was 55, a dramatic change took place. One night God appeared to him in his room, in the form of a man. He had chosen him to declare to men the spiritual contents of Scripture, he told Swedenborg, and he himself would tell him what he should write on the subject. Then, that same night, Swedenborg's spiritual eyes were opened and he was enabled to have conscious perception of the spiritual world and its inhabitants. Thereafter Swedenborg gave up all worldly pursuits and devoted himself entirely to writing about his travels in the spiritual world, where he met, and conversed with, angels, deceased human beings, and devils, and to explaining the true, spiritual meaning of the Bible in the light of the principle of correspondences, according to which everything in the material world has its counterpart in the spiritual world. Probably the best known of Swedenborg's theological writings is *Heaven and its Wonders and Hell: From Things Heard and Seen*, which I read when I was fifteen in a Penguin paperback edition. I cannot remember what I made of it then. I think I read it in the same spirit in which I read *Paradise Lost* and *The Divine Comedy*, both of which had much to say about the inhabitants of the spiritual world, both celestial and infernal. Swedenborg was buried in the Swedish Church in London, but in 1908 the Swedish government had his remains removed to Uppsala Cathedral, where they were deposited in a magnificent sarcophagus of Swedish red granite. The last time I was in Sweden I visited Uppsala, and in the gloom of the cathedral had a glimpse of the dull red bulk of the sarcophagus behind its protecting iron grille.

The lives of Swedenborg and Blake overlapped by thirty-five years. William Blake was born in 1757, and it was in this year, according to Swedenborg, that the Last Judgement took place. It took place not on earth but in the spiritual world, when all who had lived from the beginning of creation were gathered together and judged and when a New Church was instituted in the heavens. Blake was familiar with Swedenborg's writings, and annotated his own copies of several of them. Though he spoke highly of Swedenborg, calling him a 'divine teacher', and though he adopted, or adapted, many of Swedenborg's ideas, he did not hesitate to criticize him drastically or even to parody him in one of his own works. Both Blake and Swedenborg were visionaries, with this difference: that Blake not only communicated his visions in words but could also draw and paint them. Blake cannot be described as a saint or a mystic in the Christian sense of those terms, nor was he a Christian in any sense other than that which he himself attached to the word. With Blake, as with Swedenborg to a lesser degree, we pass from the Christian to the post-Christian era of European history. In the sixties and seventies I found in his poetry and his art, as well as in his life, a source of great inspiration, as did many others in those heady days. As I wrote at the time:

> A whole century before Buddhism was really known in
> the West Blake offers us the unique example of a
> non-theistic imaginative vision of rare intensity and

integrity. That he could do this was due in the first place to his own extraordinary creative powers – powers which manifested early, and of which he remained in unimpaired possession to the end of his days, he being faithful to them, and they being faithful to him.

CHAPTER
EIGHT

JESUS

THE FIRST THOUGHT THAT OCCURS TO ME as I start thinking about Jesus is that I don't have any strong feelings about him, whether positive or negative. I would not go so far as to say he leaves me cold; but he certainly leaves me feeling rather luke-warm. In my early teen years a particularly moving sermon by the pastor of the Baptist church I was attending could leave me with a heart overflowing with love for Jesus, but by the time I reached home the emotion would usually have evaporated and I was never anywhere near 'accepting Jesus as my personal saviour', as it was called, and never even thought seriously about doing such a thing.

One of the reasons why I don't have any strong feelings about Jesus is that I have never been able finally to convince myself that such a person as Jesus of Nazareth did once live as a man among men, whatever myths and legends may later have gathered around his name. At one time I would be convinced that Jesus was an historical figure; at another, that he was not. It depended on which of the many books on the subject I happened to be read-ing just then. Thus over the years my mind swung back and forth between the two alternatives at least four or five times, though without my ever having an emotional investment in either of them. Eventually I decided that it was more likely that Jesus had *not* lived than that he had, and this remained my position until fairly recently, when I happened to read about Marcion, the founder of Marcionism, who was active as a teacher in Rome between the years 150 and 160 (his date of birth is unknown). According to Marcion, Jesus was a purely spiritual being who, descending from heaven, had suddenly appeared in Galilee in the fifteenth year of the reign of the Roman emperor Tiberius.

I was at once reminded of the beginning of the Gospel According to St Mark. This gospel, the oldest of the four gospels that were to be recognized as authentic by the Catholic Church, begins by relating how Jesus came from Nazareth in Galilee to the river Jordan, there to be baptized by John the Baptist (Mark 1:9–11). It makes no mention of the antecedents of Jesus, or of what he was doing before he 'came from Nazareth of Galilee'. There is nothing about his miraculous conception, as there is in two of the other gospels, nothing about the visit of the Magi, nothing about the flight into Egypt, nothing about the massacre of the Innocents. For the author of Mark's gospel, as more explicitly for Marcion, the life of Jesus began when he suddenly appeared, not necessarily from heaven, in the Galilean town of Nazareth (thus Mark) or Capernaum (thus Marcion). Mark's gospel does, of course, refer briefly to the mother and brothers of Jesus; but Marcion would have regarded this as an example of the false Judaic traditions that had grown up around the Apostles, on account of which he had been obliged to reject *in toto* the gospels of Matthew, Mark, and John, regarding as authentic only certain parts of the gospel ascribed to Luke.

All this suggests to me that Jesus may in fact have 'appeared' from somewhere outside Palestine, perhaps even from India or Central Asia. This is no more than a hypothesis, and Christians no doubt will reject it out of hand; but I, for one, find it easier to believe that Jesus may have come from somewhere outside Palestine than that he was born of a virgin and was God incarnate. Indeed, the possibility of his having come from somewhere outside Palestine makes it more likely, in my view, that Jesus *had* lived than that he had not.

Some Christians will tell me that the truth about Jesus has been handed down within the Church, in an unbroken tradition, since the days of the Apostles, and that I ought therefore simply to accept its testimony that he was an historical figure. As a

Buddhist, or even as a thinking human being, I cannot do this. Christians of another kind will tell me that if I were to study the Four Gospels intensively I would be convinced, in the end, that Jesus really had lived. For this I have never had either the time or the interest. Or rather, I would have found the time had the interest been sufficiently strong. But for me the question of whether Jesus had or had not lived was not a pressing one, for it had no bearing on my own spiritual life as a Buddhist. Nonetheless I did once read Albert Schweitzer's *In Quest of the Historical Jesus*, a history of the critical study of the life of Jesus by a succession of nineteenth-century German scholars, for whom the existence of Jesus was a matter of religious as well as scholarly concern. Some had discovered a rational Jesus behind the gospel narratives, others a 'liberal' Jesus, and so on. Schweitzer himself opted for an eschatological Jesus, a Jesus who believed he was the Messiah and that the world would come to an end within the lifetime of the disciples; he opts for a Jesus who escapes from history, a Jesus who cannot be known historically but only as a spirit within men. For Schweitzer, the quest for the historical Jesus had ended in failure; but that did not mean that it was devoid of value, for it had shown where Jesus was *not* to be found. Indeed, Schweitzer insists that it is impossible to over-estimate the value of what German research upon the life of Jesus had accomplished. He goes so far as to call it 'a uniquely great expression of sincerity, one of the most significant events in the whole mental and spiritual life of humanity.' This is a large claim and one which to some people will seem a little Eurocentric, not to say Germanocentric.

The quest for the historical Jesus did not cease with the publication of Schweitzer's famous book. Though it seems not to have continued in Germany, it certainly continued elsewhere, if in academically less reputable quarters. In the course of the last forty years I have come across Jesus the Great Initiate, Jesus the leader of an uprising against the power of Rome, Jesus the Magician, Jesus the Socialist, the Aryan Jesus, the New Age Jesus, Jesus the Archetype of the Self, and the extraterrestrial Jesus who came from another planet and who returned there, thus explaining the Ascensions. The list is far from complete, and I am sure that as time goes on other Jesuses will be discovered, whether in the scriptures or in the depths of someone's imagination.

Although I have never made an intensive study of the Four Gospels it was inevitable that in the course of my life I should have acquired some knowledge of them, either directly or through references to them in my general reading. One does not have to read the Gospels in order to know the parables. The literature of Europe is full of allusions to them. I cannot remember when I first read, or heard, such parables as those of the Good Samaritan, the Prodigal Son, and the Mustard Seed. It is as though I had drawn them in with my earliest breath. Some parables I came to know through paintings that illustrated them. I cannot even think of the Parables as being essentially Christian. Many of them give expression to universal human values, and are independent of their immediate context in this or that gospel. A few parables, such as that of the Sower, have parallels in the Buddhist scriptures, the genre being one that was widespread in the ancient world. I regard the Parables as part of my cultural heritage as a European, and I do not hesitate to make use of them in writing for, or speaking to, a Western audience about Buddhism.

Just as one doesn't have to read the Gospels in order to know the Parables, so one does not need to read them in order to familiarize oneself with the sayings of Jesus. These pithy utterances, too, are part of European literature. Such sayings as 'No man can serve two masters,' 'Judge not that ye be not judged,' and 'By their fruits ye shall know them,' stuck in my mind, though I do not know when I first heard them or read them, and could not say offhand just where in the Gospels they are to be found. They stuck in my mind partly because they reached me in the language of the Authorized Version, which is more forceful, direct, and concise than that of more recent translations of the Bible. As the Buddha's poet-disciple Vangisa chanted in the Master's presence, 'Truth verily is immortal speech' – which I take to mean that truth is made memorable when it finds poetic expression. In the case of some of the sayings I felt there was a living individual behind them, giving emphatic utterance to his thoughts and feelings. But whether that same individual was also behind all the other sayings, discourses, diatribes, and prophecies ascribed to Jesus by the authors of the Four Gospels was quite another matter.

Besides telling us what Jesus said, the Gospels also tell us what he did. One of the things he did was perform miracles, a miracle being defined, in this connection, as 'an effect above human or natural power, performed in attestation of some truth' (Johnson). The truth to which the miracles of the Gospels attest is that Jesus possesses Divine authority. Most of the miracles are miracles of healing, the healing sometimes involving the casting out of a demon who has taken possession of the sick person. There were also cases of what we would call faith healing, as when a woman who had suffered from a haemorrhage for twelve years came up behind Jesus in the crowd and touched his garment, thinking that could she but touch his clothes she would be cured. She was instantly cured, and Jesus told her, 'Daughter, thy faith hath made thee whole' (Mark 5:34). There is also the curious episode in which Jesus, on a visit to Nazareth, his home town, was unable to work any miracle there, though he cured a few sick people by laying his hands on them. The author of the Gospel comments that Jesus 'marvelled because of their unbelief', or as a modern translation has it, 'was amazed at their lack of faith' (Mark 6:6). Another class of miracles demonstrates that Jesus has power over the elements. He calms a storm (Mark 4:39–40), feeds five thousand people with five loaves and two fish (Matthew 14:19–20), turns water into wine (John 2:1–11), and raises Lazarus from the dead (John 11:11–44).

How do I, as a Buddhist, view these miracles? I certainly believe there is such a thing as faith healing, a form of treatment not, however, to be confused with spiritual healing, which takes place *without* the need for faith on the part of the patient. I therefore see no reason why Jesus, had such a person existed, could not have performed miracles of this kind. Unlike the authors of the Gospels, and unlike Christians down to our own times, I do not regard them as miracles in the sense defined above and not, therefore, as attesting to the possession by Jesus, or any other faith healer, of Divine authority. Similarly I see no reason why Jesus could not have calmed a storm. The art of weather-making is still known to certain Tibetan lamas, one of whom, a friend of mine, once told that it was relatively easy to stop rain from falling on a particular spot but quite difficult to conjure it from a clear blue sky. On the turning of water into wine I have an open mind. There could be a natural explanation (Schweitzer gives one), or, alternatively, it could have involved the use of psychic powers not unknown to the yogins of India and Tibet. The raising of Lazarus from the dead is a miracle of a radically different kind. So far as I know, it is beyond human power to bring back to life a man who is really dead, especially when he has been dead four days, as Lazarus had, and 'stinketh' (John 11:39). It is possible for one to believe that Jesus literally raised Lazarus from the dead only if one believes that Jesus was God Incarnate, and as such had power over death. Since I cannot believe, as the Christian does, that Jesus was God Incarnate (for as a Buddhist I do not believe in the existence of God), I cannot believe, either, that Jesus once brought a dead man back to life. The author of John's gospel evidently included this miracle in his narrative in attestation of the Divine status and authority of Jesus, and it is significant that he chose to locate it shortly before Jesus's own death and resurrection.

From debates about whether or not Jesus had really lived, and about the reliability or otherwise of the Gospel narratives, I have at times turned with relief to Jesus as depicted in Christian art. The Christian artist believed in the existence of Jesus, just as he believed, *as an artist*, in the existence of the gods and goddesses of pagan antiquity when, with the dawn of the Renaissance, he came to depict them, too. He did not know what Jesus had looked like any more than he knew how Mars and Venus looked. In the Christian art of the fourth to the twelfth centuries there is in any case little attempt at realism. Attitudes tend to be stiff and hieratic, as they still are in Orthodox religious art, and Jesus is sometimes depicted as a beardless youth, as in the mosaics at Ravenna, sometimes as a bearded man of mature years, as in the mosaics of certain basilica churches in Rome. As art became more realistic, the artists attempted to give Jesus a consistent, recogniz-able individual character, as Duccio does in the panels illustrating the life of the Saviour in his *Maestà* in the cathedral museum of Siena, and as Giotto does to an even greater degree in his frescoes in the Arena Chapel in Padua. In the latter series it is very much the same Jesus who attends the marriage at Cana in one fresco, and who in others raises Lazarus from the dead, enters Jerusalem riding on a donkey, and expels the merchants from the Temple. He is a handsome, dignified man in the prime of life, with brown hair and beard. His expression is calm, his gesture hieratic. Even when being crowned with thorns, in another fresco, he remains impassive, simply half-closing his eyes. It is only in the fresco of the Crucifixion that, with eyes now closed, and head fallen to one side, that he shows any sign of suffering – a suffering Giotto has the good taste not to exploit in the way some later artists were to do.

With Masaccio, a hundred years after Giotto, Jesus becomes more statuesque, occupying not two-dimensional but three-dimensional space, as do the disciples. He is depicted with them in Masaccio's finest work, his fresco in the Brancacci Chapel, Florence, illustrat-ing the miracle of the tax money, part of which I saw when the chapel was undergoing restoration. The circumstances of the miracle are described in the Gospel According to St Matthew, and only there, and were as follows. Jesus and his disciples were stay-ing at Capernaum. There the collector of the Temple tax asked St Peter if his master paid the tax. When St Peter told Jesus this the latter directed him to cast a hook in the lake, take the first fish that bit, and open its mouth. There he would find a piece of money, which he was to give to the tax collector for the two of them (Matthew 17:24–7). In the fresco Jesus occupies the centre of the composition. The disciples stand in a semi-circle round him, and he is flanked by St Peter on the left and by the tax collector on the right. Jesus, his right arm extended, points to St Peter, who, extending *his* right arm in a vigorous gesture which continues that of the Master, points to a small, crouching figure at the extreme left of the fresco who was taking something from the mouth of a fish. The small figure is St Peter himself, for Masaccio has united the three parts of the episode in a single scene, the third part being that in which, at the extreme right of the fresco, St Peter gives the money into the hand of the tax collector. The weakest part of the fresco, unfortunately, is the head of Jesus, now widely attributed to Masolino. One critic goes so far as to describe it as doll-like and lifeless compared to the heads of the disciples. He finds it difficult, he says, to imagine Masaccio conceiving Divinity in terms so mild and dreamy.

But why did Masaccio not paint the head of Jesus himself, thus putting the finishing touch to his masterpiece? This was the question that puzzled me as I studied a small reproduction of the fresco. Did Masaccio die before he was able to complete his fresco by painting the head of Jesus? Or did Masolino insist that he, as the older and more experienced artist, ought to do the work? So far as I am aware, there is no evidence to support either of these theories, though it is known that Masaccio died young, at the age of twenty-six, not in Florence but in Rome, allegedly by poisoning. My own explanation of the mystery is not circumstantial but psychological. According to the critic to whom I have referred above, the head of Jesus in the fresco is doll-like and lifeless *compared to the heads of the disciples*. The latter are, in fact, very finely portrayed. This is particularly true of the head of St Peter. His hair and beard are grizzled, the corners of his mouth are turned down, and he glares rather than looks at Jesus. He is evidently an irascible old man, and one possessed of great force of character. Masaccio seems to have seen into St Peter's soul. He must have asked himself what sort of man St Peter was. He must have pondered deeply on those passages in the Gospels and in the Acts of the Apostles where the saint plays a part and then have portrayed him in accordance with the impression he received. Why, then, did he not do the same in the case of Jesus? My belief is that he wanted to do so but found he was unable to see into the soul of Jesus as he had seen into St Peter's. The Four Gospels do not give, between them, a very consistent picture of the character of Jesus, and Masaccio must have found it no less difficult to make up his mind what sort of man Jesus was than have many others since his time. The question was complicated by the fact that Jesus was not just a man. For Masaccio, as a Christian, Jesus was God Incarnate, the Word that had been made flesh and had dwelt among us. How could such a being be portrayed? An artist of Masaccio's genius could not be content simply to portray Jesus as other artists had portrayed him. He must therefore have thrown down his brushes in despair and left the work of painting the head of Jesus to Masolino.

There is, perhaps, a more prosaic explanation of the mystery. It may be that Masaccio was accustomed to paint from the live model. With the growth of realism in art the practice must have been fairly widespread by this time. Perhaps Masaccio painted his portraits of the disciples from beggars he brought in from the street, just as El Greco, two centuries later, painted *his* portraits of the disciples from the inmates of the local lunatic asylum, and perhaps he had been unable to find anyone from whom he could paint the portrait of Jesus.

Though the artists of the Renaissance and the Baroque period might idealize the features of the models from whom they painted their biblical personages, the latter often show traces of the national or regional provenance of their real-life originals. Thus we have Virgins who are really Italian peasant women holding a fat Italian baby and Jesuses who are really Spanish patricians in oriental costume. Nowadays we also have the blond, blue-eyed Nordic Jesus, and the almond-eyed Chinese Jesus who, as I recently saw, rides into Jerusalem on a donkey to be welcomed by the city's almond-eyed inhabitants. There are also those artists who sought – with or without the help a model – to penetrate into the character of Jesus, as I believe Masaccio had wanted to do. Leonardo da Vinci was such an artist, his genius being one that delighted in exploring what was mysterious and unfathomable. Though it seems he hardly ever drew or painted the adult Jesus, it is the figure of Jesus that occupies the central position in what is probably his greatest work, the wall-painting of the Last Supper in the refectory of Santa Maria delle Grazie, Milan. Jesus has just told the disciples that one of them will betray him (Luke 22:21–3), and Leonardo shows them reacting in their different ways, each in accordance with his individual character. He sits with arms spread wide, hands resting palms uppermost on the table. His head is turned a little to one side and his eyes are half closed. There is no halo, but his head, with its long hair, is framed by the rectangular window immediately behind him. Time has not dealt kindly with the painting, and it is not easy to see what Leonardo made of the character of Jesus. Moreover, according to Vasari Leonardo did not 'perfect' the head of Jesus as he could not find a model that could express 'that beauty and celestial grace'. However, there exists, in Milan, a pastel head of Jesus that appears to be a study for the Last Supper. So expressive is it of that 'beauty and celestial grace' for which Leonardo sought that I find it difficult to believe that Leonardo drew the head from a model, however much he might have idealized the features. Leonardo must have sought – and found – that beauty and celestial grace in the depths of his own soul.

There are those artists, again, who were concerned not so much to penetrate into the character of Jesus as to depict the main incidents of his life in as dramatic a manner as possible. One of the most eminent of these was Tintoretto. The paintings in which he tells the gospel story from the Annunciation to the Ascension are the glory of the Scuola di San Rocco in Venice and the fullest expression of Tintoretto's extraordinary genius. Some paintings contain dozens of figures, and much movement, and Tintoretto breaks many compositional rules, so that at first glance it is difficult to make out what is happening, as I found when I visited the Scuola twenty or more years ago. I nonetheless have the distinct recollection of two of the paintings, one depicting the Temptation, the other Jesus before Pilate. In the first painting there are only two figures. Jesus is seated at the top right under the dark, unevenly projecting beams of what appears to be a roof; his head is surrounded by a mild luminescence, against which his features show in profile. From the bottom left springs a young, epicene Satan, mockingly holding up two stones, one in each hand, tempting Jesus to turn them into bread. The other painting contains a number of figures, but it is the slim, silent figure of Jesus that dominates the scene. Wrapped in a white mantle that trails down the steps, he stands like a column of light against a dark architectural background, his head bowed. A red-robed Pilate, seated in the shadows a step or two higher than Jesus, washes his hands of responsibility for the prisoner's death, which has been loudly demanded by the assembled Jews with shouts of 'Crucify him!' (Mark 15:12–14).

Several films of the life of Jesus have been made, but I have seen only one of them. This was Pasolini's *The Gospel According to St Matthew*, with background music from Bach's *St Matthew Passion*, which I saw shortly after its London release. Pasolini was said to be a devout Roman Catholic, but I could more easily have believed him to be a militant atheist. As I commented afterwards to the friend with whom I saw the film, it was as though Pasolini was saying, 'Look, I've told the story of Jesus as convincingly as I could, sticking close to the gospel narrative – but how can anyone believe it?'

Besides encountering Jesus in churches and art galleries, and at the cinema, I also encountered him in literature. When I was sixteen or seventeen I read Scholem Asch's *The Nazarene*, a novelistic version of the life of Jesus written from a Jewish point of view. It was a substantial work, but all I can remember of it is the passage in which Jesus, on a visit to a cosmopolitan coastal city, is shocked by the nudity he sees there – an illustration of the difference between Hellenic and Hebraic culture. Much more recently I read George Moore's *The Brook Kerith*, which likewise is a novelistic version of the life of Jesus. Beautifully written, from the standpoint of a non-believer with a sympathetic interest in modernist theology, it is one of the Irish author's finest works. The Jesus of *The Brook Kerith* is an Essene, a member of a Jewish sect or brotherhood that lived in the region of the Dead Sea, practising asceticism and awaiting the coming of the Messiah. Next to Jesus, the most important character in the novel is Joseph of Arimathea, with an account of whose early history the story begins. Though strongly attracted to the miracle-working preacher who claimed to be the Messiah, about whom he has heard from the fisherman who worked for his father, a pious Jew in the fish-salting trade, he does not become a disciple as he is reluctant to sell all that he has and give the proceeds to the poor as Jesus demands. Instead, he carries on his father's fish-salting business and becomes friends with the cultivated ruler of Roman Palestine, Pontius Pilate. Thus he is in a position, a few years later, to rescue the body of Jesus from the Cross for burial.

Late that night, to Joseph's astonishment, the body shows signs of life. Jesus has not died on the Cross, but he is severely trauma-tized, and it is many months before the careful nursing of Joseph and his woman-servant restores him to health. Moore's lengthy description of Jesus's gradual recovery is not only very convin-cing but extremely moving. From Joseph's house the erstwhile Messiah returns to the Essene monastery beside the Brook Kerith from whence he originally came, and shortly afterwards Joseph himself is murdered by a Zealot, a fanatical anti-Roman Jewish nationalist. But though physically healed, mentally Jesus is in a state of shock. He remains in that state for fifteen years, saying lit-tle, and living mainly by himself as an Essene shepherd in the hills. When he finally emerges from his silence it is with the real-ization that his Messiahship was a delusion and his former teach-ing harsh and cruel.

At this point, some twenty years after the Crucifixion, Paul appears on the scene. He is on his way to Rome, having been arrested for causing a riot in Jerusalem, and having appealed, as a Roman citizen, from Jewish law to the law of Rome. His guard has granted him leave from prison while he is waiting for the ship that will take him to Rome for his trial, but he and his companion are pursued by a band of Zealots and Paul, separated from his companion in the night, finds refuge in a cliff-side cave with the very sect of Essenes that has for shepherd Jesus of Nazareth. There he harangues the Essenes at great length, telling them how he was a Jew of scrupulous orthodoxy, how he cruelly persecuted the Christians, as the followers of Jesus of Nazareth were called, how that same Jesus appeared to him in a vision, and how, since then, he has travelled the world proclaiming the joyful tidings that Jesus Christ, who was crucified under Pontius Pilate, was raised by God from the dead, and that only through faith in him could anyone be saved. When Jesus arrives later and assures Paul that he did not die on the Cross, Paul does not believe him. His Jesus and the shepherd Jesus are not the same man, he thinks, though both come from Nazareth, and in any case Jesus is a common enough name.

The following day, when Jesus guides Paul through the desert to a point from where he can see the port which is his destination, he again tries to convince him that there is only one Jesus of Nazareth, that he is that Jesus, and that he did not perish on the Cross; but this time Paul thinks he must be out of his wits or that he is a demon come to tempt him. However, he asks Jesus what thoughts came to him in the hills, and Jesus tells him. Shortly after they part Paul sees people in a strange garb going towards the hillside on which he has left Jesus. They are monks from India, a shepherd informs him. Paul sees the likeness between the thoughts Jesus has confided to him and the shepherd's account of the doctrines that were being preached by the monks from India. The monks will meet Jesus in the valley, Paul muses, 'and if they speak to him they will soon gather from him that he divined much of their philosophy by watching his flock, and finding him of their mind they may ask him to return to India with them and he will preach there.'

CHAPTER
NINE

BARLAAM AND JOSAPHAT

THERE IS A SCENE in the *Merchant of Venice* in which the suitors of Portia, a spirited young heiress, are shown three caskets, one of gold, one of silver, and one of lead. One of them contains Portia's portrait, and according to her father's will the suitor who chooses the right casket, the one containing the portrait, will be able to marry Portia. The Prince of Morocco chooses the gold casket, but on opening it he finds only a skeleton and some verses beginning

> All that glitters is not gold;
> Often have you heard that told.

Similarly the Prince of Aragon, on being shown the caskets, chooses the silver one and to his chagrin finds the portrait of a 'blinking idiot' and some sardonic verses. The third suitor is Bassanio, a young Venetian with whom Portia herself is secretly in love. He chooses the lead casket, where he finds Portia's portrait and verses inviting him to claim the lady 'with a loving kiss'. Few of those who have seen the play will have known that Shakespeare took the theme of the Three Caskets from the romance of Barlaam and Josaphat, a Christianized version of episodes from the life of the Buddha, which he found in *The Golden Legend* (1483), Caxton's version of a French translation of the *Legenda Aurea*, a work compiled in Latin by the thirteenth-century Dominican friar Jacobus de Voragine who became Archbishop of Geneva.

The story of the monk Barlaam and prince Josaphat underwent many changes before eventually passing from Voragine to

Caxton and from Caxton to Shakespeare, but in Caxton's English version, still very readable, incidents which are parts of the Buddha's biography as handed down in Buddhist tradition can nevertheless still be discerned. The story begins in a legendary India, which is represented as being 'full of Christians and of monks'. At this time there arose a powerful king named Avennir who persecuted the Christians, and especially the monks. Nonetheless, a friend of the king who was also his chief minister was inspired to leave the palace and become a monk. When the king heard of this he was beside himself with rage and ordered a search to be made for the monk, who was eventually found and brought before the king. On seeing his former minister 'in a vile coat and much lean for hunger' Avennir called him fool and madman and wanted to know why he had changed his honour into disgrace and made himself a mockery. If he was willing to listen to reason, the monk replied, then he should put from him his enemies. The king naturally wanted to know who his enemies were. They were anger and greed, the monk explained, for they obscured and hindered the mind, so that the truth might not be seen. 'The fools despise the things that be', the monk continued, 'like as they were not, and he that hath not the taste of the things that be, he shall not use the sweetness of them, and may not learn the truth of them that be not.'

I was greatly struck by these words. Behind them, beneath all the layers of adaptation and modification, I could see an important teaching of the Buddha that must have come from one of the traditional Indian biographies. The spiritually immature despise the real because they see it as unreal; and he that has no experience of the real will not benefit from the happiness it brings, nor, since he sees the real as unreal, will he see the unreal as unreal. This is reminiscent of a verse in one of the best known Buddhist scriptures: 'Those who, having known the real (*sara*) as the real, and the unreal (*asara*) as the unreal, they, moving in the sphere of right thought, will attain the real' (*Dhammapada* 12). Whoever was originally responsible for this version of the story of Barlaam and Josaphat must have felt that the monk's teaching to the king was not particularly Christian, as indeed it is not, for he credits the

monk with having gone on to 'show many things of mystery of
the incarnation', which is obviously out of place and very likely
was added at some stage. Be that as it may, Avennir was not impressed by the monk's teaching. Had he not promised to put
away anger, he tells him, he would have burned him alive. Let
him go now, lest he should do him some harm.

Meanwhile, it so happened that a son was born to the king, who
hitherto had been childless. The boy was called Josaphat, which
is not really a proper name but the form assumed by the Sanskrit
word 'bodhisattva' after it had been transcribed from the alpha-
bet of one language into that of another, and from that into yet
another, thus becoming a little further removed from its original
spelling and pronunciation each time. In the traditional
biographies the term 'Bodhisattva' refers to the Buddha in the
pre-Enlightenment phase of his career, the word meaning
'Enlightenment-being' or 'one bent on Enlightenment'. On the
birth of Josaphat 'the king assembled a right great company of
people for to sacrifice to his gods for the nativity of his son, and
also assembled fifty-five astronomers, of whom he enquired what
should befall of his son.' In the *Abhiniṣkramaṇa Sūtra* or 'Sūtra of
the Great Renunciation', one of the canonical biographies of the
Buddha, the astrologers assembled by King Suddhodana, the
Bodhisattva's father, predicts that his son will become either a
universal monarch or a Buddha, an Enlightened One. A sage
who has arrived from the Himalayas, however, predicts that he
will definitely become a Buddha. King Avennir's astronomers tell
him that Josaphat will be 'great in power and in riches'; but one of
them, wiser than the others, predicts that the child will be a Christian, a member of the religion that the king persecutes. Disturbed
by the prediction, Avennir took measures to ensure that Josaphat
does not hear about Jesus Christ. They are the same measures
taken by Suddhodana, in the traditional biographies of the
Buddha, to ensure that Siddhartha does not learn about the real-
ities of human existence. In Caxton's words:

> And when the king heard that, he doubted much, and did
> do make without the city a right noble palace, and therein

set he his son for to dwell and abide, and set there right fair younglings, and commanded them that they should not speak to him of death, ne of old age, ne of sickness, ne of poverty, ne of no thing that may give him cause of heaviness, but say to him all things that be joyous, so that his mind may be esprised with gladness, and that he think on nothing to come. And anon as any of his servants were sick the king commanded for to take them away, and set another, whole, in his stead, and commanded that no mention should be made to him of Jesus Christ.

Except for the reference to Jesus, the Buddhist will find himself on familiar ground here. He will also know what follows. But at this point the story of Barlaam and Josaphat, as translated by Caxton, is interrupted by a tale of palace intrigue, in which King Avennir tries to trick his chief noble into admitting that he was a Christian by telling him that he has decided to become a monk, and in which the noble tricks the king, and saves his own life, by becoming a monk in order, as he says, to accompany the king into the desert and serve him there. The story is then resumed, and the Buddhist again finds himself on familiar ground. When Josaphat grew up he wondered why his father had so enclosed him, and became greatly depressed that he could not go out. On hearing this the king made arrangements for 'horses and joyful fellowship' to accompany him, but in such a way that he should see no distressing sight.

And on a time thus as the king's son went, he met a mesel (leper) and a blind man, and when he saw them he was abashed, and enquired what them ailed, and his servants said: These be passions (sufferings) that come to men. And he demanded if those passions come to all men, and they said: Nay. Then said he: Be they known which men shall suffer these passions without definition? And they answered: Who is he that may know the adventures of men? And he began to be much anguishous for the incustomable thing thereof. And another time he found a man much aged which had his cheer (face) frounced (wrinkled), his teeth fallen, and was all crooked for age. Whereof he was abashed, and he desired to know the miracle of this vision. And when he knew that this was because he had lived many years, then he demanded what should be the end, and they said: Death; and he said: Is then death the end of all men or of some? And they said for certain that all men must die. And when he knew that all should die, he demanded them in how many years that should happen, and they said: In old age or four score years or a hundred, and after that age the death followeth. And this young man remembered oft in his heart these things, and was in great discomfort, but he showed him much glad tofore his father, and he desired much to be informed and taught in these things.

Josaphat has now seen the first two, and heard about the third, of the Four Sights that are described at length, and with a wealth of detail, in the traditional biographies of the Buddha; but he has yet to see the fourth sight, that of a monk. In the story of Barlaam and Josaphat it naturally is a Christian monk that he meets. The monk's name is Barlaam. The derivation of the name is uncertain: it may be a corrupt form of the Sanskrit word *bhagavan*, meaning 'lord'. Barlaam is described as 'a monk of perfect life and good opinion that dwelled in the desert of the land of Senaar'. Coming to know about Josaphat by divine inspiration, he disguised himself as a merchant and gained access to him by telling 'the greatest governor of the king's son' that he had a miraculous precious stone to sell and wished to offer it to the prince. The governor wanted to see the precious stone, but on hearing that it could be safely seen only by one who was wholly chaste he changed his mind and brought him to Josaphat, who received him honourably. Barlaam told him he did well in taking no heed of his 'littleness that appeareth withoutforth'. He was like the king whose barons were displeased with him for getting down from his chariot and humbly saluting to poor men, thus compromising his royal dignity. In order to teach them a lesson the king ordered four chests to be made. Two of the chests he covered with gold and jewels and filled and with dead men's bones and filth. The other two he covered with pitch and filled with precious jewels and rich gems. Here we obviously have the originals of the Three Caskets in *The Merchant of Venice*, where despite his more romantic handling of the theme Shakespeare draws much the same moral as Barlaam, who continues:

> And after this the king do call his great barons ... and did do set these four chests tofore them, and demanded of them which were most precious, and they said that the two that were gilt were most of value. Then the king commanded that they should be opened, and anon a great stench issued out of them. And the king said: They are like them that be clothed with precious vestments and be full withinforth of ordure and of sin. And after he made open the other and there issued a marvellous sweet odour. And after, the king said: These be semblable to the poor men that I met and honoured, for though they be clad in foul vestments, yet shine they withinforth with good odour of good virtues, and ye take none heed but to that withoutforth, and consider not what is within.

Having related this apologue, Barlaam preached Josaphat a long sermon about the creation of the world, about the day of judgement, and about the reward of good and evil. This he followed up with a series of apologues, some of them quite amusing, on the foolishness of idol worship, the fallaciousness of worldly pleasure, the difference between true and false friendship, and the inevitability of death. Several of the apologues have, to me, a familiar, almost Buddhistic ring to them, especially the one on true and false friendship. There was a man who had three friends. He loved the first friend as much as himself, the second less than himself, the third little or naught. It so happened that this man was in danger of his life, and was summoned before the king. He ran for help to his first friend, reminding him how much he had always loved him. But the friend refused to help, saying he had to spend the day with other friends, and in any case he did not know him. The man went sadly to his second friend, who excused himself from accompanying him to the king, saying he had many responsibilities; but he would accompany him as far as the palace gate. At last the man went to his third friend. 'I have no reason to speak to thee,' he admitted, 'ne I have not loved thee as I ought, but I am in tribulation and without friends, and pray thee that thou help me.' The third friend readily agreed to the man's request, saying, 'I confess to be thy dear friend and have not forgotten the little benefit thou hast done to me, and I shall go right gladly with thee tofore the king, for to see what shall be demanded of thee, and I shall pray the king for thee.' The first friend, Barlaam explained, was possession of riches, for the sake of which man puts himself in many dangers, and of which he can take with him, when death comes, only the winding sheet in which he will be buried. The second friend was his sons, his wife, and his kin, who can go with him only as far as his grave, after which they will return home and get on with their own lives. The third friend was faith, hope, and charity, and other good works we have done, which when we leave our bodies may go before us and pray for us to God, and may deliver us from our enemies the devils.

The first time I read this apologue, in Caxton's English version, it at once put me in mind of the old morality play of *Everyman* which I saw at a London theatre during the War. This ballet moved me more deeply than had the play on which it was based, with which I was already familiar. On the drop curtain Blake's 'Ancient of Days', enormously enlarged, bent over the Deep with his compasses creating the world. Then, out of the darkness, came a tremendous voice, declaring:

> I behold here in my majesty
> How that all beings be to me unkind,
> Living without fear in worldly prosperity,
> On earthly treasure is all their mind.

God therefore sends a messenger to Everyman, requiring him to appear before him. The 'mighty messenger' is Death. On receiving the message Everyman runs in turn to his friends Fellowship, Kindred, Cousin, and Goods, but none is willing to go with him on his journey. At length he calls out to his Good Deeds, asking her where she is. But she is 'called in ground', his sins having bound her so tightly that she is unable to move. He releases her, and she goes with him on his journey, as does Knowledge, to whom the play's unknown author gives the memorable lines:

> Everyman, I will go with thee and be thy guide,
> In thy most need to go by thy side.

The play may be derived from a Dutch close counterpart, as one scholar believes; or, alternatively, it may be based on Barlaam's apologue on true and false friendship, publication of *The Golden Legend* having preceded the composition of *Everyman* by about twenty-five years. In any case, the play is a work of something like genius and must have touched the hearts of the audience for which it was written, including as it does a universal truth – the truth that 'you can't take it with you'.

When he had been fully instructed by Barlaam, Josaphat wanted to leave his father and follow the monk. Barlaam approved his resolution, and to illustrate it he related another apologue; but he did not agree that Josaphat should follow him into the desert. Instead, he should wait until it was the right time for them to meet. He then baptized Josaphat and 'returned into his cell'. Shortly afterwards Avennir heard that his son had become a Christian. On the advice of his friend Arachis he sought out an old pagan hermit who resembled Barlaam and instructed him to engage in public debate with the pagan masters. First he should defend the Christian faith, then allow himself to be defeated by the arguments of the pagans and revert to paganism. In this way Josaphat would lose faith in Christianity and follow suit. But Josaphat was not deceived. He told the false Barlaam, whose name was Nachor, that if he was defeated by the pagan masters he would, when he became king, tear out his tongue with his own hands for having dared to teach a king's son a false religion. Judging that he had more to fear from the son than from the father, who had promised him immunity whatever the result of the debate, he attacked the gods of paganism with great vigour.

The Chaldees worshipped the elements, the Greeks worshipped gods and goddesses who were guilty of the grossest immorality, and the Egyptians worshipped animals, whereas Christians worshipped 'the son of the right high king that descended from heaven and took nature human'. He then defended Christianity so clearly and convincingly that the pagan masters were discomfited and did not know what to say. Josaphat was overjoyed at the false Barlaam's victory. He told him privately that he knew who he really was, converted him to Christianity, and sent him into the desert, where he was baptized and led the life of a hermit.

On coming to hear of these things an enchanter named Theodosius approached the king and advised him to take away his son's present attendants and replace them with beautiful, well-adorned women who should be instructed never to leave the prince, for 'there is nothing that may so soon deceive the young man as the beauty of women'. He would then send to the prince an evil spirit who would inflame his mind with lust. The king did what the enchanter advised, but when Josaphat felt himself to be inwardly burning with lust he prayed to God for help, whereupon all temptation left him. The king then sent to him a beautiful young princess who was fatherless. Josaphat preached to her and she promised to become a Christian if he would marry her. When he refused she promised that if he would lie with her for only that night she would become a Christian in the morning, arguing that according to his own religion 'the angels have more joy in heaven of one sinner doing penance than on many others'. Seeing how strongly the woman was assailing Josaphat the devils came to her aid, so that the prince's fleshly craving incited him to sin at the same time that he desired the woman's salvation. Weeping, he betook himself to prayer, fell asleep, and 'saw by a vision that he was brought into a meadow arrayed with fair flowers, there where the leaves of the trees demened a sweet sound which came by a wind agreeable, and thereout issued a marvellous odour, and the fruit was right fair to see, and right delectable of taste, and there were seats of gold and silver and precious stones, and the beds were noble and preciously adorned, and right clear water ran thereby'. He then entered into a city the walls of which were of fine gold, and where he saw in the air 'some that sang a song that never ear of mortal man heard like'. This, he was told, was the abode of the blessed saints. He then was shown a horrible place full of filth and stench, and told this was the abode of the wicked. When Josaphat awoke, it seemed to him that 'the beauty of the damosel was more foul and stinking than all other ordure'.

Despairing of ever being able to persuade his son to abjure Christianity, King Avennir made over to him half his kingdom, though Josaphat desired with all his heart to go and live in the desert. For the sake of spreading his faith, however, he consented to rule for a while, and built churches, and raised crosses, and converted many people to Christianity, including his own father, who after leaving the whole kingdom to his son engaged in works of penance. Josaphat himself, after ruling for much longer than he wanted, at last fled away into the desert, 'and as he went in a desert he gave to a poor man his habit royal and abode in a right poor gown', just as the Bodhisattva, in one of the traditional biographies of the Buddha, exchanges his princely robes for the saffron-coloured dress of a huntsman. What directly follows is reminiscent of the Bodhisattva's defeat of Māra, prior to his attaining Enlightenment, except that Josaphat prays to God whereas the Bodhisattva relies on his own inner resources.

> And the devil made to him many assaults, for sometimes he ran upon him with a sword drawn and menaced to smite if he left not the desert; and another time he appeared to him in the form of a wild beast and foamed and ran on him as he would have devoured him, and then Josaphat said: Our Lord is mine helper. I doubt no thing that man may do to me.

Josaphat then spent two years wandering in the desert looking for Barlaam. At last he found a cave in the earth, knocked at the door, and said, 'Father, bless me.'

> And anon Barlaam heard the voice of him, and rose up
> and went out, and then each kissed other and embraced
> straitly and were glad of their assembling.

Afterwards Josaphat told Barlaam all that had happened to him since they parted. Barlaam died in the year 408 AD, the story goes on to relate. As for Josaphat, he left his kingdom in his twenty-fifth year, and lived the life of a hermit for thirty-five years, and was buried by the body of Barlaam. On hearing of this, King Barachius, who it seems had been left in charge of the kingdom, removed the bodies of the two saints to his city, where their tomb was the scene of many miracles.

Just as Caxton translated the story of Barlaam and Josaphat from Voragine's Latin version, via the French, Voragine himself drew his material from an earlier source, that drew from one still earlier, and so on through layer upon layer of different languages and cultures back to the Sanskrit text with which the whole process began. Scholars have not been able to identify this urtext, as it may be called, but it must have been related to such works as the *Lalitavistara* and the *Buddhacarita*. In any case, it was freely translated or adapted into Pehlevi in Central Asia under Manichean auspices, the prophet Mani, the third-century founder of Manicheism, having regarded the Buddha as God's messenger to India, just as Zarathustra was his messenger to Persia, Jesus his messenger to the West, and Mani himself his messenger to Babylonia. This Pehlevi version, which appears to be no longer extant, was translated into Arabic probably in the eighth century by an unknown author and still survives. Under the title of *The Book of Balawha and Budasf* the Arabic version became popular in the Islamic world, and gave rise to numerous abridgements and adaptations in the same language. It also was the basis of the various Greek, Christianized versions of the story, the last and most highly embellished recension of which appeared in the ninth century and was later attributed to St John of Damascus, the last of the Greek Fathers. Versions of the Arabic work appeared not only in Greek but also in Hebrew, Persian, and Georgian.

So far as Western Europe is concerned, the most important of the versions deriving from *The Book of Balawha and Budasf* is the one attributed to St John of Damascus, for it was from this version that the Latin translations of the Middle Ages were all made. The first of the extant translations appears to have been made in the twelfth century. Other translations followed, including that of Jacobus de Voragine, which was the source not only of Caxton's English version of the story of Barlaam and Josaphat but also of versions in French, German, Italian, Spanish, Portuguese, Swedish, Icelandic, Irish, and a number of other languages. The abundance of these versions testifies to the popularity of the story through the Middle Ages and well into the Renaissance period. Caxton's version of the *Legenda Aurea*, of which the story of Barlaam and Josaphat forms a part, was his most popular publication. It was often reprinted, and a copy of the work must have fallen into Shakespeare's hands before he came to write *The Merchant of Venice*, which was between 1596 and 1598.

There were two main reasons for the widespread popularity of the romantic story of the young prince who, having lived a life of enforced seclusion, was suddenly confronted by the facts of human existence and became a monk. In the first place, the story of Barlaam and Josaphat as it stands now is a good read. It has been described as 'a strange mixture of parable and fable, of folklore and history, and romance, in which shrewd worldly wisdom is mingled with the highest and greatest religious truths in such a way that the perusal thereof will increase the piety of the godly, the wisdom of the wise, and the pleasure of those who seek amusement and instruction in the writings of teachers of olden times'. Secondly, the story was set in the distant, mysterious, almost mythical land of India, about whose geographical location most people in the Middle Ages had only the vaguest of ideas. According to Christian tradition St Thomas, one of the twelve apostles, travelled to India not long after the death of Jesus and converted the whole country to Christianity. In the course of time it slipped back into paganism and it was Barlaam and Josaphat who, between them, reconverted the land to the true faith. For this pious work, as well as for the holiness of their lives, the two saints were greatly honoured by both the Eastern Orthodox Church and the Western Church, Barlaam and Josaphat being commemorated by the Roman Catholic Church on 27 November, while the Greek Church commemorates Josaphat by himself on 26 August and the Georgian Church Barlaam by himself on 19 May. In the Russian Church Barlaam and Josaphat, together with the latter's father King Avennir, are all commemorated on 19 November, though this day properly belongs to St Barlaam of Antioch, an early Christian martyr.

To the best of my knowledge, no churches were dedicated to Barlaam and Josaphat, nor do they feature in the religious art of the Middle Ages and the Renaissance, though it may well be that paintings illustrating their story are hidden away in remote churches and obscure provincial art galleries. Despite this apparent neglect, there are probably churches where their feast days are still celebrated, and where neither priest nor people realize that in venerating Barlaam and Josaphat they are in fact honouring the Buddha and the unknown Indian ascetic who, as the last of the Four Sights, had inspired the young Siddhartha to go forth from home in quest of Enlightenment.

CHAPTER
TEN

BUDDHISM AND CHRISTIANITY

FOR THE LAST NINE MONTHS I HAVE SPENT much of my time thinking and writing about the contact I have had with Christianity and Christians in the course of the last eighty years. This is the longest time I have ever spent immersed in the religion into which I was born (or at least baptized), and to which I never really belonged, and those who have followed me thus far may want to know what I have learnt from the experience. Have I changed my ideas about Christianity, or about Buddhism, or about the relation between the two religions? Have I learned anything about myself? I do not think I have learned from my immersion in Christianity anything that I did not know before, but it certainly helped me to see more clearly, and feel more deeply, some of the things I already knew, and for this reason I believe the experience to have been worthwhile. Though I was not in a position to embark on a systematic comparative study of Buddhism and Christianity, which in any case would have been an immense undertaking, such limited comparisons as I was able to make were sufficient to highlight the fundamental differences that exist between the two religions.

The fact that there are such differences, not only between Buddhism and Christianity but also between them and other religions, and between the other religions themselves, at once gives rise to certain questions. How, for instance, can people of different religious beliefs live together in peace and harmony, or at least without overt conflict? One answer is that this happy state of affairs would be achieved if everybody were to believe that religions were in essence the same, or that they all lead ultimately to the same goal. Neither orthodox Buddhists nor orthodox Christians would agree that religions are, in fact, the same in essence, or that they all lead ultimately to the same goal, and this has been my position, too, ever since I started thinking seriously about the Buddha's teaching. But at this point Buddhists and Christians part company. According to Buddhism, it is possible for one to be convinced of the truth of one's own faith and yet, at the same time, to feel no hatred for those who think differently. Indeed, for one who is a Buddhist it is desirable, even imperative, that he should have towards those of other faiths an attitude not of hatred but of positive goodwill, for hatred is an obstacle on the path to Enlightenment, besides being disruptive of that sense of natural solidarity with other human beings on which ethics is based. Judging by the way the Church has treated heretics and non-believers when it was in a position of power, Christians believe that conviction of the truth of one's own faith is not incompatible with hatred for those who think differently. Indeed, many Christians seem to have believed that it was good and right, and pleasing to God, that they should, as a natural expression of their faith, hate and persecute pagans and heretics.

I have always been aware of the Christian record in this respect, but as a result of my recent immersion in Christianity, especially in its Roman Catholic form, I have become more aware of what that record tells us about the nature of Christianity. Like most other people, I tended to regard such phenomena as the Inquisition and the Crusades as unfortunate episodes in European history, regrettable mainly on account of the tens of thousands of human lives they had brought to an untimely end. The officers of the Inquisition, in conjunction with the secular authorities, sent men and women to the stake because they refused to believe as the Church believed. The Crusaders slew Muslims because they were followers of a different religion. As I reflected on these things, I felt more deeply than ever the enormity of religious intolerance, springing as it does from an unholy alliance of ignorance, hatred, and fear. I thought of the lonely death of the Bohemian reformer Jan Hus, sent to the stake by the Council of Constance in 1415 as a heretic for attacking the ecclesiastical abuses and rejecting the pope's authority. I recalled seeing, in the Prado, Berruguete's famous painting of St Dominic presiding over the burning of heretics, in the bottom right hand corner of which two naked, anonymous victims of the Inquisition are seen fastened to posts, ready for burning, while St Dominic, seated aloft beneath a huge canopy, his throne surrounded by clerical and lay dignitaries, calmly presides over the proceedings. I also bethought me of the two hundred and more *perfecti* who, after the surrender of the great Cathar fortress of Montségur in 1244, were thrust into a wooded palisade with combustible material and burnt.

Jan Hus, the anonymous victims of the Inquisition, and the two hundred and more Cathar *perfecti*, as well as tens of thousands of other heretics, were all *burnt alive*, thus suffering one of the most horrible of deaths. These burnings took place under the auspices of the highest religious and secular authorities; they were justified by theologians, approved by saints and mystics, and applauded by ordinary people. Apologists for Christianity have naturally sought to minimize the significance of the burnings, arguing that the number of victims has been exaggerated, or that Christianity has done more good in the world that harm, or that what men did in the Middle Ages is not to be judged by modern standards. I find none of these arguments convincing. Nothing can minimize the horror of a man or woman being burnt alive for believing differently from the rest of the community. It was not that the officers of the Inquisition, for example, necessarily enjoyed their work, or that they became Inquisitors because it put them in the position of being able to inflict pain and suffering on others. For the most part they seem to have been learned and pious men who were determined to stamp out heresy and who believed that in burning heretics they were doing their duty by God and man. If they ever felt pity for the sufferings of their victims they would probably have stifled the feeling, regarding it as being inspired by the Devil. There would seem to be in the very nature of Christianity a strand of intolerance that is capable of overriding all considerations of common humanity. In the course of recent months I have become more aware of this deadly strand, and more aware of the difference, in this and other respects, between Buddhism and Christianity.

Though I have spoken of my being immersed in *Christianity*, I have in fact often been immersed in Roman Catholicism, this being the form of Christianity that has played a dominant part in the political and economic life of Western Europe, as well as in its religious and cultural life. It is no accident that Roman Catholicism is so called. It is the Roman Catholic Church itself that is the true legatee of the Roman Empire, not the so-called Holy Roman Empire, for it was the Roman Church which for a thousand years – from the sack of Rome by the Goths to the Reformation – provided the iron framework that helped to hold the peoples of Western Europe together as the religio-political entity known as Christendom, of which the pope was the supreme head and ultimate authority. This iron framework prevented Western Europe from falling into chaos, and to this extent it was a good thing, as I saw more clearly as I renewed my acquaintance with the history of Western Europe during the period of papal ascendancy. But although that iron framework helped to ensure a degree of social and political stability and cohesion, intellectually and spiritually it was often constrictive, and to this extent it was a bad thing. At its most constrictive, intellectually and spiritually speaking, it could be destructive not only of independent thought but of life as in its treatment of heresy and heretics.

In every generation there were, however, men and women who, while the rest were content to live out their lives within the framework, contrived to find, or make, little openings in it, through which they could get a glimpse of the wider world outside. There were others who made use of it for their own purposes, whether noble or ignoble, creative or exploitive. Among these were the poets and artists, especially the artists. The framework consisted not only of dogmas and laws; myths, symbols, and sacred history were also part of it. Provided he respected certain conventions, the artist was free to depict a subject taken from the Bible, or the legends of the saints, or ecclesiastical history, in accordance with the dictates of his own genius. If he painted a picture of St Jerome in his study, for example, he would almost certainly have included the saint's broad-brimmed cardinal's hat, and the hat would have been red, not any other colour; but such details as the dimensions of the study, the nature of its furniture, how it was lighted, and whether or not St Jerome was half naked, or had a long white beard, were all left to the discretion and taste of the artist – unless the individual or community commissioning the painting had some wishes in this connection, in which case he would have respected them just as he respected the conventions laid down by the Church. Altogether there must be scores, even hundreds, of such paintings of St Jerome, all making use of at least some of the traditional iconographic elements but all differing in style and treatment. From the best of these we learn less about St Jerome than about the character, temperament, and depth of insight of the artist himself. A painting of St Jerome in his study may be not so much a Christian work of art as a manifestation of human creativity, as may a painting of a subject taken from the Bible, or the lives of the saints, or ecclesiastical tradition.

This is why I am able, though a Buddhist, to appreciate and enjoy, even to be deeply moved by, what is best and greatest in Christian art, as well as what is best and greatest in Christian poetry and music. In this I am not alone among Western Buddhists, some of whom would say that it was only after becoming Buddhists that they learned to appreciate Christian art. A Christian painting contains no overt doctrinal element, which would be repugnant to me; for viewed simply as a painting it does not contain, and cannot contain, any conceptual element. On the other hand, a Christian musical composition, such as Bach's Mass in B Minor or Handel's *Messiah*, does contain a doctrinal element, inasmuch as it is a setting to music of the words of a certain religious text, in which case I can either ignore the words (this is easier if they are in a language I do not understand) or mentally give them a Buddhist application. A Christian poem consists of words, as does any poem, and some of these words will be expressive of concepts, including doctrinal concepts. If the poem happens to be a narrative one, like *Paradise Lost* or the *Divine Comedy*, the doctrinal concepts will be part of the story, like Homer's assertions about his gods and goddesses in the *Iliad* and the *Odyssey*, and their presence therefore does not obstruct my enjoyment of the poem.

It is because I distinguish between Christianity and Christian culture, and see the latter as owing far more to human genius than to the teaching of the Church, that I am able, though a Buddhist, to appreciate and enjoy the 'Christian' art, music, and poetry of the West. I am thus in a paradoxical position. As a Buddhist, I reject Christian doctrine, but as a Westerner I am able to appreciate and enjoy 'Christian' culture. But I am a *Western* Buddhist. Though I accept the Buddha's teaching, which comes to me from the East, as a Westerner I do not feel as much 'at home' with Eastern Buddhist culture, whether Sinhalese, Thai, or Tibetan, as one brought up within it. Moreover, although there is Western Buddhism, in the sense that there are tens of thousands of Europeans and Americans who regard themselves as Buddhists, there is no such thing as a Western Buddhist culture. I can therefore well understand the feelings of the English academic who, having converted back to Catholicism after twenty-five years as a member of a Tibetan Buddhist group, was delighted to find himself surrounded, in his native land, by the cathedrals, pilgrimage sites, and other holy places of his religion. As a Western Buddhist, I am not similarly situated. The English landscape is not dotted with stupas and mani walls and other reminders of the Dharma. My practice of the Dharma does not have the support of an indigenous Buddhist culture.

But things will change. I am confident that the next hundred years will see the beginnings of an indigenous Western Buddhist culture. A few green shoots have already appeared here and there. But even when we have our own Western Buddhist culture many Western Buddhists will continue to enjoy the poetry, music, and art of the old 'Christian' culture. Meanwhile, now that I have finished recalling, and reflecting upon, my personal contact with Christianity and Christians, I cannot but feel that it is infinitely better for me to be a Western Buddhist without a culture of his own than a Christian with one.

INDEX

A

Abhiniṣkramaṇa Sūtra 155
Aelred of Rievaulx 112
Albigensians 69
Alexander VI 122
alternative Christianity 69
angels 73ff, 80ff, 135
animals 101
Annunciation 90
Apostles' Creed 49ff, 55, 67
Aquinas, St Thomas 42
Aristotle 42
art 63, 77, 84, 94, 127, 144, 147, 170ff
    see also cinema, fresco,
    literature, painting
Ascension 63, 141
Assumption 91
Athanasian Creed 67
avatāra 56
Avennir 154ff

B

baptismal creed
    see Apostles' Creed
Barlaam 153ff
Bernard of Clairvaux, St 27, 124
Bhagavadgītā 56, 122
Bible 107, 117, 130, 135
    as literature 17ff
    (see also individual books)
Blake William 17, 72, 82, 136ff
bodhicitta 76, 77
bodhisattva 76, 81, 155
bonfire of vanities 121

Boys' Brigade 10, 102
Bridget of Sweden, St 134
Bruno, St 125
Buddha 56f, 58f, 112, 122, 154, 157, 162
Buddhism 35, 60, 65, 97ff, 130
    supression 45ff
Bunyan, John 12
burning 32ff, 68f, 87, 168, 169
Butler, Samuel 14

C

Carthusian order 125
Cathars 69
Catherine of Siena, St 130ff
Caxton, William 154ff, 163
Christ *see* Jesus
Church 31ff *and passim*
Church of England 49
cinema 149
Cistercian order 124
Clement VII 34, 133
confession 42
Congregational Church 7
consciousness 53
Constantine I 33, 35, 68, 116
Constantinople 94, 116
conversion 40, 120, 161, 164
Creation 52ff
creed
    Apostles' 49ff, 55, 67
    Athanasian 67
    Epiphanius 64
    Nicene 51, 54f, 68ff

crucifixion 58, 65, 90, 117, 127ff, 145, 150

crusade 29, 47, 116, 125, 133, 168

D

Dante Alighieri 36, 72, 83, 92, 108

death 159

deva 75, 81

devil 84ff, 161f, *see also* Satan

Dhammapada 65, 66, 154

Dharmakāya 76

di Tondo, Niccolà 133

Diamond Sūtra 16

Dionysius 75

Dominic, St 169

Dormition 91

E

Eastern Orthodox Church 46

ego 123

Elizabeth I 31ff

Enlightenment 53, 58, 76, 97

Epiphanius, Creed of 64

ethics 67, 97ff, *see also* morality

Everyman 159

excommunication 36, 39, 68

execution 122, 127, 134

   see also burning, crucifixion

Exodus 107

F

faith 58, 143

forgiveness 65, 107

Four Sights 157

Francis of Assisi 14, 119

Franciscans 113

fresco 83, 88, 131, 134, 145

friendship 79, 111ff, 158

G

Gadarene swine 85

Gibbon, Edward 14

Giotto di Bondone 84, 145

God 17, 51, 54, 63, 116, 122,

   see also theism

Great Schism 37

Gregory XI 132, 133

guardian angel 80ff

guilt 100ff, 128

Guyon, Jeanne 119

H

Hamlet 62

healing 143

heaven 63

hell 59ff, 66, 81, 83, 92, 108, 124

Henry VIII 34, 126

heretic 68, 70, 87, 113, 114, 124, 168ff

Hinduism 56

historicity 57ff, 67, 139ff

Holy Ghost 7, 54, 63ff, 68, 90

homosexuality 2, 103ff

Huxley, Aldous 29

I

imagination 71

India 40ff, 90, 151, 154, 164

injustice 101

Inquisition 31, 33, 50, 114, 168

interfaith groups 47

intolerance 113, 116ff, 168f

Irenaeus 87, 115

Isaiah 64

Islam 80, 133, 168

J

Jerome, St 128ff, 171

Jesuit 42

Jesus 36, 51, 54, 57, 58, 85, 107f, 139ff

Jews 18, 27

Job 17ff, 64

John the Baptist 55, 127, 140

John, St, Gospel of 65, 90, 115, 144

Josaphat 153ff

Joseph of Arimathea 149
Judaism 115
Judges, Book of 29
judgement 107, 121
    Last 60, 63, 83, 125, 136
Jung, C.G. 129
justice 20, 60, *see also* punishment

K
Kakacūpama Sutta 66
Kalimpong 40, 124
karma 60, 66, 101
killing (of animals) 101
    see also execution
King John 36ff

L
Last Judgement 60, 63, 83, 125, 136
Lawrence of the Resurrection 122
Lawrence, St 127
Lazarus 63, 144
Lefebvre, Marcel 40
Leonardo da Vinci 147
Leviathan 24
Leviticus 104, 106
literature 9, 17ff, 71ff, 75, 94, 119ff,
    136, 149
Lord's Prayer 66
Lourdes 92
Lucifer 81, *see also* Satan
Luke, St, Gospel of 117, 140

M
Mangala Sutta 75
Māra 162, *see also* devil
Marcion 117, 139
Mark, St, Gospel of 60, 84, 140
martyrs 126
Masaccio 145
Mascarenhas, Father 41
massacre 32, 69
Matthew, St, Gospel of 60, 108, 145

Merchant of Venice 153, 158
Merton, Thomas 123
Messiah 54
Michelangelo 60
Milton, John 10, 36, 69, 71, 73, 80ff,
    86
miracle 55, 85, 143ff, 163
missionaries 40
Monchanin, Father 41
Moore, George 149
morality 115, 132, *see also* ethics
music 171
Muslims 133, 168
mysticism 27, 119ff, 121ff
mythology 63, 71ff, 80

N
Nicene Creed 51, 54f, 68ff

O
Origen 61, 124
original sin 65

P
Pachomius, St 124
paganism 86, 87, 115, 160, 164, 168
painting 6, 9, 74, 78ff, 88ff, 127, 147
parables 8, 142
Paul, St 61, 86, 87, 98, 104, 150
Pentecost 64
persecution 113
Peter, St 36, 64, 115, 145
Philip II 31, 37, 114
pigs 85
Pius II 134
Pius V 32
Pontius Pilate 57, 150
pope 35ff, 133,
    (see also individual popes)
power 35, 38ff, 47
Prajñāpāramitā 95
prayer 5, 11, 107, 131

precepts 101
prophesy 64
Protestantism 34, 98
Proverbs, Book of 27
Psalms, Book of 27
punishment 20, 66,
    see also execution, justice

Q
Quakers 113
Quietism 121

R
redemption 57
Resurrection 55, 63
Revelation, Book of 13, 39
Ridolfi Plot 31
Robinson, John 46
Roman Catholicism 33, 40, 47, 68,
    170 *and passim*
Romans, Epistle to 104, 106
Russian Orthodox Church 94ff

S
saint 119ff
    (see also individual saints)
Samuel, Books of 29
sangha 113
Śaṅkara 42
Satan 18, 38, 73, 81ff, 87, 148,
    see also devil
Savonarola, Girolamo 34, 121
Schweitzer, Albert 141
self-immolation 45
Sermon on the Mount 67, 107
sex 102ff
Shakespeare, William 37, 62, 71,
    153, 158, 164
Silvester I 35, 38

sin 62, 65, 106, 128
Song of Solomon 17, 25ff
Sophia 94
Spanish Armada 31, 37
suffering 18, *see also* punishment
Sunday School 6ff
Swedenborg, Emanuel 135

T
Ten Commandments 98
theism 46, *see also* God
theology 118
Theosophy 14
Thich Quong Duc 45
Thomas Aquinas, St 14
Thomas, St 164
Tintoretto 148
Tobias 78
Tobit, Book of 78
transubstantiation 69
Trinity 54, 64, 67

U
Urban VI 133, 134

V
Vietnam 44
violence *see* burning, execution,
    intolerance, killing, massacre,
    punishment
Virgil 108
Virgin Mary 55ff, 89ff
Voltaire, Françoise de 14

W
Wadia, Sophia 42
Waldensians 69
Wilde, Oscar 103
witches 107
Woolwich, Bishop of 46